making
# kimono
& japanese clothes

# CONTENTS

# INTRODUCTION
# A brief history of the kimono

When westerners first arrived in Japan and enquired the name of the clothing, they were told 'kimono' – which literally means 'thing to wear'! Kimono was thus a generic word that embraced a whole range of garments, but gradually it has come to refer to the full-length robe, made from straight strips of cloth, that people the world over would recognize. It is a word, like 'sheep' and 'fish', that has the same form for both singular and plural uses.

Early in Japanese history, people were much influenced by contact with China, wearing Chinese-style robes and adopting the Chinese hierarchy of colours for rulers and court officials. During the Nara period (AD 710–794), however, garments resembling the kimono began to appear and, after Japan suspended contact with China (one of several such episodes), a style began to emerge that became uniquely Japanese.

Kimono were generally worn in layers, each carefully cut to reveal a glimpse of colour, the layers being sequenced and coordinated to suit the season. At a time roughly similar to the mediaeval period in Europe, court ladies would wear twelve or more robes at a time, this conspicuous consumption proving that one could afford to sustain the lifestyle of the court. Sleeves also went through a period of being far more enormous than a sleeve actually needs to be. This compares with court fashions in Europe at late mediaeval times, where the same ostentatious display of wealth in costume similarly represented power and authority. Just as in Europe, too, this was a period in which heraldry was highly developed and socially important. Your family crest, or kamon (see page 20), was displayed on your clothes, your household effects and the livery worn by your household servants.

*Right* A 20th-century recreation of the multi-layered Heian ensemble worn by court ladies of the period.

*Left* Embroidery enriches this print with satin stitch and couched gold thread.

Eventually the number of layers in an ensemble settled down to about five. However, in the cold of winter one might wear more, and sometimes the relative coldness of winters was described in terms of the number of kimono that had been needed! Despite this, the average kimono was not usually padded, although the silk robes worn at court were usually lined, especially those intended for winter wear (with lining colours also carefully specified to suit the ensemble).

The most familiar form of the kimono is based upon a version called a kosode, which translates as 'small sleeves'. Japanese girls and young women used to wear flowing sleeves, sometimes to floor length, in a style called furisode. Such sleeves were considered to be tools of flirtation because they could be waved about to catch the eyes of young men. Consequently, upon marriage, these sleeves had to be cut off short. A beautiful sample of embroidery, featured on page 81, is actually just such a cut-off sleeve. As women grew older, therefore, their sleeves were worn shorter, and the colours they chose also became more subdued.

If you ever have the chance to study a genuine kimono (in other words, not the sort sold in department stores for tourists), take it. It will be a tremendous opportunity to learn about both textile decoration and the construction of these historic garments. I once received a box of kimono pieces which came indirectly from a Japanese 'Lady'. Inside the box were a number of pieces that clearly came from the same garment and I realized there was perhaps a chance to reassemble the whole. In the event, a few bits

*Left* This detail shows several 'tide-pools' of colour with resist-dyed motifs, flowing freely over woven geometric and floral motifs in the background silk.

*Left* This Showa-period kimono displays typical decorative features composed in an asymmetrical yet balanced way. Note the scattered embroidered accents: colourful plum blossoms and maple leaves in metallic thread.

were missing. Where the panels had been unpicked, tiny strands of silk sometimes remained, and the distinctive marks of the running stitches that had originally held all together could still be seen. Matching their subtle variations showed whether the correct two seams were being joined.

On the reverse of the fabric, itself a beautiful putty-coloured silk jacquard, were hand-drawn pencil marks. These marks sketched out the areas to be dyed with various pools of colour. Still visible were the characters specifying the shades: 'white', for example, or 'rust' or 'purple'. This showed that the garment had been a bespoke piece of dyeing. On the right side, the fabric was decorated with painted or dyed sprays of flowers and so forth, some of which had been embellished further with satin stitch or metallic thread embroidery. This kimono was probably produced by a workshop that offered the skills of many individuals, and it was made using very traditional methods, including assembly by hand, at a time well after the introduction of the sewing machine. The garment may date from early in the Showa period (1926–89).

On one sleeve, I noticed a very small kamon, the crest of the lady's family. It is a pair of crossed arrow feathers, suggesting that maybe this was the emblem of a military family. Studying the remaining panels more closely, I found another in the corresponding position on the other sleeve. A third was placed at the centre back, worked so that when the back seam was stitched the two parts would come together correctly. The kamon have been worked in metallic thread, and the three would have appeared in line with each other across the back of the wearer. Their presence indicates that the garment was intended for formal occasions. There is only one higher degree of

*Left* What a thrill to discover finely pencilled lines and characters instructing the craftsmen where to place the colours. Enjoy the delicately shaded foliage forms.

*Right*  This discreet rendition of a kamon, embroidered in fine metallic thread, measures barely 2.5cm (1in) in diameter.

formality, represented by kimono bearing five crests. As the wearing of kamon was abolished at the end of World War II, the garment must pre-date this time.

For a modern Japanese woman, the choice of kimono comes loaded with meaning: for example, how formal the garment is, therefore when it should be worn, and details about the age or marital status of the wearer. It is no wonder that the majority of Japanese took to western dress eventually, as it allows women to be far more discreet about such personal facts.

There are many conventions to the wearing of today's kimono, which is chiefly a stylized version of the garments and dress codes of the former samurai class. It is a complete outfit, and the wearer will generally require help to put it on, as well as instruction in the correct deportment when wearing it. Considering the long history of this garment, it is sad that, for many modern Japanese women, the only time they will don a complete kimono ensemble is on their wedding day.

Nevertheless, there is a survivor from the kimono camp, namely the yukata. This word describes both the kind of fabric used to make it – typically a crisp indigo-dyed cotton – and the style of unlined kimono made with it. This is worn by both men and women as informal leisurewear and is the equivalent of the tracksuit or T-shirt and shorts that westerners might put on after work to relax in during a summer's evening. As such, it provides a departure point for the basic kimono that you can make and enjoy for yourself.

If this brief history of the kimono has inspired you to know more about Japanese clothing, suggested titles for further reading can be found in the Bibliography.

# Using this book

Targeted at the enthusiastic home stitcher and dressmaker, this book aims to present simple, easy-to-sew garments, derived from traditional Japanese clothing. It is not about the production of historically accurate ensembles from specific periods of Japanese history nor about the present-day, highly stylized version of the kimono which, though beautiful to look at, is scarcely practical for life in the 21st century.

Starting with the kimono, the form of which lends itself so well to all manner of decorative techniques, we progress through interpretations of other traditional Japanese garments that can readily find a place in the flexible wardrobes of both men and women. These are all simple shapes that make up into classic and timeless garments. With that in mind, consider fabric choices carefully – you could find yourself wearing a favourite for a long time! Do not feel that you must seek out fabric that 'looks Japanese' – unless that is what you truly want. My opinion, for what it is worth, is that these garments will all work best in classic materials that will not readily date, such as silk and linen. If that sounds limited, also consider ethnic textiles. Often decorated in a bold way, they are well displayed by the large garment panels and they also will not seem tied to a particular period in fashion. If fabrics have been produced by traditional methods, expect variations in dyeing or printing and note that the finished article may be more likely to shed colour when washed. Accept these in the Japanese spirit, as a natural consequence of the way they are made and expressing the touch of the maker.

As an item of leisurewear, the kimono is potentially much more than the dressing gown so often seen in lingerie departments. Returning home to shower after work or a sports session, the kimono is the perfect garment to put on, whether you are male or female. You can feel comfortable, yet presentable enough to welcome unexpected visitors.

The jacket and trouser options may be interpreted in very diverse fabrics, to make either smart evening outfits or casual combinations for your next holiday. There need be no fancy construction processes, no mastering buttonholes or inserting zippers if you're new to dressmaking. Yet if you're a craftsperson, the basic panels may be decorative masterpieces.

Your decoration may be inspired by anything you choose, but in case you want to maintain a Japanese theme, there are notes on design and use of colour, and some accessible decorative techniques are described. It seems that many craftspeople turn to Japanese garments as a place to display their particular skill because these simple clothes are not demanding to construct. Indeed, this may be why you yourself purchased this book.

Our ideas relate to observations of genuine Japanese garments and textile techniques. These have been translated for the modern maker, who may not have much time and is perhaps only just discovering the joys of personalizing clothing. Most chapters describe decorative details used in the sample garments. Some include guidance intended to help those readers who are novices to dressmaking to get started. More detailed instructions appear in Chapter 2.

Naturally, techniques are not tied to specific garments and must be considered as basic methods, intended to inspire you to your own inventions. Employ skills you already have or be motivated to learn something new!

**Please read the rest of this introduction before using the patterns in the book as it explains their presentation and gives general advice.**

# The patterns

Each pattern chapter (3–9) covers a different item or group of variations on the basic theme, including a descriptive introduction and an illustration of the original Japanese garment that was used as the source for the relevant pattern. The kimono does not have a paper pattern, being simply cut as rectangles of cloth.

## Patterns and sizing

Japanese traditional clothing is not sized in the way that westerners are accustomed to, whether buying ready-made clothes or paper patterns for home dressmaking. The basic dimensions were governed by the width of cloth usually produced, approximately 35cm (14in), and fit was simply achieved by taking more or less seam allowance as required. Traditional clothes were hand-sewn with running stitches and were taken apart for laundering, being tacked (basted) back together into a continuous length for this process! Needless to say, laundering didn't happen very often and sometimes lengths were not reassembled for the same owner. However, because the fabric had not been cut into elaborate pieces with one size in mind, the lengths could be made into a garment for someone else of rather different dimensions and there was no waste.

It is an interesting idea and, while not likely to be copied in modern wear, it is worth remembering that fit is a relative concept. However, most women's garments comfortably fit UK sizes 12–14, USA 10–12. The men's jimbei and waistcoat fit chest 112cm (44in). As most garment panels are more-or-less rectangles, I suggest that you assess your measurements against the dimensions of the panels you will be drafting and make simple straight seam adjustments whenever appropriate. For a garment such as the mompe, it is worth making a trial version from inexpensive fabric.

## Materials and cutting notes

There are suggested quantities of fabric for each pattern as given, usually in typical western widths, but sometimes also with lengths based on the narrow Japanese fabric of 35cm (14in).

However, there is an old saying about thrift which refers to the need 'to cut one's coat according to one's cloth', and this is never more appropriate, nor more easy to attempt, than when applied to garments inspired by the Japanese tradition. Further advice on fabric cutting modifications appears on page 14.

## Assembly instructions

The assembly instructions assume some sewing skill. They hopefully strike a balance between being simple to follow while providing more detail for steps which may be unfamiliar. I have been struck by the general simplicity of construction of the Japanese clothes that I have seen, but do not let the simple approach trick you into thinking that this means poorly made. For the most part, traditional Japanese clothes were very well made, sometimes with exquisite detailing. The overall attitude towards execution seems to have been 'as simple as possible, as beautiful as possible'.

# General sewing information

## Pattern cutting

The patterns are scaled down to fit the pages of the book, so you will need to draft them to the full size for yourself. For this, you will require a sharp pencil, a long ruler or yardstick and squared paper. Dressmaker's paper with 5cm (2in) squares is best. If this is not available, you will also need a set (try) square or square quilter's rule to draw accurate right angles.

A routine way to work is to begin with the centre back seam and hence the back panel of the garment. Usually the draft progresses to the front of the garment, followed by the sleeves, and then extras such as collars or ties.

A few pieces, for example the armhole on the western-style waistcoat, require the drawing of a curve. This is aided by drawing a diagonal line along which a measurement can be marked. You then plot the curve by connecting the marked point to the straight lines on each side of it. Similarly on the back neck of the waistcoat, two lines at right angles mark where the back rises to cover the shoulders and a free curve can be drawn within.

Copy labelling and cutting notes from pattern diagrams, marking dots or notches. They will help you to make up the garment correctly and easily.

After drafting and before cutting any fabric, check the pieces against one another. If two pieces are to be sewn together, they should obviously be the same length. This quick check can reveal errors in pattern pieces before you proceed to cut your precious fabric. Similarly, if you adjust the length, perhaps to fit a garment into less fabric, check that all relevant pieces are treated the same.

Less experienced makers may like to make a test garment from inexpensive fabric, such as muslin (cheesecloth) or lining, to see what the fit will be like and how the pieces go together. Transfer adjustments made to this practice garment, called a 'toile', back to the master pattern. Again, take care to modify all seams that sew together in a like manner. Keep the toile for other people to try on: if someone asks you to make a similar garment for them, this will allow you to see what changes need to be made.

By comparing the pattern from one garment with another, you will find that some are so similar that a toile will not be needed for every variation.

## Fabric cutting

Every effort has been made to provide accurate estimates with the garments, but if in doubt, always buy a little more fabric than you think you may need. Please note that for several garments, quantities are given for traditional Japanese-width cloth as well as standard western widths. Japanese cloth is narrow – only 35cm (14in) approximately – and therefore in many cases only one pattern piece can be fitted into the width. Consequently, the amount required sounds like a great deal more than you may expect. It also means that most garments made from traditional Japanese fabric have a centre back seam. This has been included in patterns where Japanese fabric is more likely to be used. If you choose western fabric widths and want to avoid the seam, you must place the pattern piece to a fold, but with the seam allowance removed or projecting 1.5cm (⅝in) beyond the fold so that it is not included. If you forget, you will have a garment that is 3cm (1¼in) bigger round the body – which you may not feel is a problem in a jacket or coat. However, the back neck may seem unusually wide and the collar will appear to be short of the hemline on the jacket or coat front – perhaps less desirable consequences.

Another convention in Japanese construction is to have no shoulder seam. This is done by cutting the back and front in one single length. However, if you have a fabric with a direction, such as flowers growing up a trellis, you will probably prefer to cut the fabric the correct way up on both back and front. You will therefore need to divide the pattern along the shoulder line and add 1.5cm (⅝in) seam allowances to both back and front shoulder seams.

These facts help to make devising a definite cutting layout for any garment quite challenging. Whatever guidance is shown, you may feel that a different layout would suit your fabric better.

To devise your own, begin with the largest pieces first and note those which you want to be placed on a fold. It may be best to fold the fabric lengthways for only just enough width to accommodate the back piece; cut this out, and then refold it horizontally for cutting the collar front and sleeves. Lay the pattern pieces on your fabric, marking their outlines with pins, and see whether you can make the pieces fit. You can often reduce the width of a panel by, say 1cm (⅜in), on vertical body seams without much impact on appearance or comfort. Lengths can be adjusted often with even less impact.

The major points to be aware of when devising one's own layouts are:

a) to treat matching or joining seams or edges the same: if you are shortening a garment, reduce all panels by the same amount; if you are changing the width, take an equal amount off at side seams on both back and front;
b) to check panels that need cutting for left and right sides, such as with the waistcoat, to obtain both;
c) always to check that there will be enough fabric for two of everything that needs two and that folds are where they should be.

Usually, minor pieces will come from the scraps, but if you are really short of fabric, find a substitute. Go for a colour match if you like, or be creative with a contrast.

If the fabric that you want to use is very expensive, you can work out the most economical layout by marking out a floor area to the correct width and using that to create the best layout before purchasing.

When you have worked out your layout and checked that all the required pieces are fitted in, pin the pattern pieces thoroughly and cut out carefully. Do not rush. Pay attention to what you are doing. Try not to 'over-cut' into the space surrounding the piece you are cutting, especially if you have had to put the pieces together snugly or if you plan to refold the fabric for cutting subsequent pieces. Careless over-cutting can scupper a carefully calculated plan – please heed the voice of experience!

Before removing the paper patterns, transfer all markings to the fabric layers.

# Marking methods

For a beginner, this task can be a puzzle, as there is no single method that will suit all situations in terms of fabric type and technique being used.

## To transfer pattern markings

Use a dressmaker's pencil (see below) to draw, say, a short line across a seam allowance to show the centre or where another edge must match, or to mark a dot as a point to which to sew.

When expensive fabrics are being used for special projects, tailor tacks are best way to transfer pattern markings. With double thread in the needle, insert it at the point to be marked, taking it through the pattern and all fabric layers. At the back, leave a generous loop before reinserting the needle in almost the same place. Make another large loop on top as you take the needle to the back again. Cut the thread, leaving a tail. When all required points are marked, ease away the pattern without losing the loops. Separate the fabric layers carefully, leaving equal lengths of thread for each layer, and cut the thread through the centre point between the fabric layers.

To mark the positioning of pockets and so on, tailor tacks at the corners will suffice. Remove tacks as you proceed with the stitching.

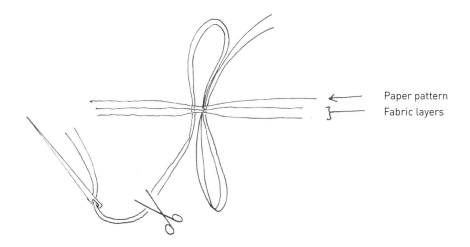

Paper pattern
Fabric layers

# Marking decorative motifs or designs

Marking a design is simplest when you have a light background fabric. If possible, work over a light surface. Place the design underneath the ironed fabric and you can usually see it well enough to trace. If not, a light box or improvized equivalent, such as taping your fabric against a window, will do the job.

The obvious tool for tracing is a pencil. A fine-line, medium-to-hard variety is best and a self-sharpening version is available as a quilter's pencil. Avoid drawing solid lines all round any design. Too often, something refuses to fit as it should, resulting in marks remaining visible. Instead, mark important corners or junctions in the design and make just a faint line of dashes between them. Pencil marks need to be washed out, though this sometimes takes more than one attempt, so it is not a good idea to use pencil to mark a fabric sold as dry-clean only, such as silk.

Dressmaker's pencils come in colours such as white, pink, light blue, lemon and silver. They are rather chalky in texture and don't sharpen to such a fine point as graphite, making the line thicker. Perhaps silver is most versatile, as it shows up on most fabrics.

The blue wash-away marker is widely available but will not show up on dark fabrics. Use this carefully – if you accidentally iron over the marks, they become fixed and will no longer wash away! Leaving the work in strong sunlight can have the same result. When the work is complete, ensure markings are washed away thoroughly. Although spraying with water will disperse markings enough for you to think they are gone, the chemicals are still present in the fibres and may reappear on the surface later. This type of marker also has a 'relative' – the fade-away marker. The slight disadvantage here is that if you do not finish the work promptly enough, the design may fade away too quickly.

To mark simple designs of straight lines, try craft masking tape, readily available from quilting suppliers.

Designs such as sashiko, often worked in white thread on navy (indigo) fabric, cannot be traced onto dark fabrics from a master laid below. One method that you can use in such cases is to place a sheet of light-coloured dressmaker's carbon next to the fabric, with the pattern over both, and then trace the design, using a hera (a curved marking tool available from most haberdashers) or an exhausted ballpoint pen. The hera is preferable, as it is less likely to tear the pattern.

An alternative method is known as 'prick and pounce'. Pierce the paper design with holes, either by hand, with a needle, or more speedily by sewing with an unthreaded sewing machine. Place the marked pattern over the right side of the fabric, holding the two together with pins or paperclips, and then cover with fine powder – either chalk as sold for the purpose or talcum powder. Gently (to avoid moving the design), rub the chalk into the holes with a pad of cotton wool. Peep underneath to check that the design is marked fully before removing the pattern. The design now needs outlining with a light marker, such as silver pencil, because the little points of talc will soon vanish.

# General sewing advice

It is expected that you will use a sewing machine when making your garments. Therefore, when the instructions say 'sew' or 'stitch', this usually means on the machine.

Before starting, decide whether you prefer to hand-finish some steps as invisibly as possible or whether they will be machine topstitched. Either is satisfactory, but it is sensible to be consistent within a project.

When the instructions say 'hand sew' or 'hand finish', load a needle with matching thread and sew with slip stitch/blind stitch, as shown, as invisibly as possible. Usually this will be to secure something, such as the turned edge of a collar, where the stitches should pass from the folded edge of the collar into the machine stitching which has attached the other edge. Sometimes, you will be sewing into the main fabric of the garment itself, for example when stitching a hem. Aim to catch only a few threads of the weave, stitching so lightly that the needle does not penetrate to the right side and thus leaves no visible marks.

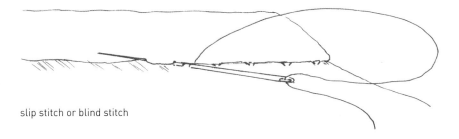

slip stitch or blind stitch

Before beginning, check that your machine is clean and in working order. Acquire the habit of 'new project, new needle', keeping a small supply of different sizes in your accessory box. Choose a needle size to suit the fabric you are using: fine needles, such as no. 70 (size 10) for silks; no. 80 (size 12) for cottons and heavier silk, such as noil, and no. 90 (size 14) for denim and heavier fabrics.

Sew a sample of two layers of your fabric with the chosen thread to check which needle to use and make any necessary adjustments to the tension. Correct tension is when the top and bottom threads meet in the middle of the two layers. Check with your manual for making adjustments.

Most of the allowances included in pattern drafts are 1.5cm (⅝in), the width used for all main garment seams. Modern machines may well have markings printed on the throat plate to guide a consistent width. This seam allowance is common on commercial garment patterns, but in a number of places, such as where facings are attached, it is trimmed to reduce bulk. The patterns given here therefore adopt the simpler method of giving 1cm (⅜in) allowances on such edges as collars and even 5mm (¼in) on some turned items, such as ties. This means you do not need to spend time trimming. The majority of seams on Japanese garments are straight or almost straight, so only very rarely will you find the instruction to 'clip the curve'. To do this, cut into the seam allowance at right angles to its edge, cutting towards the stitching line but stopping about 3mm (⅛in) before the stitches. This helps the layers lie flat when turned right side out.

Most garments with sleeves imitate the kimono style, so you do not have to 'set in' sleeves, as is common with western patterns. Instead, you sew the sleeve to the body along a dropped shoulder-line. To make the following side and underarm seams easier to sew, it helps if you do not sew right across the seam allowances. Instead, mark where the seam allowances come, then start and stop sewing at the beginning and end exactly. To strengthen the beginning and end of the stitching, either reverse-sew a little or use the '0' stitch length setting to sew a few stitches on the spot. Return to a normal stitch length (10 stitches per 2.5cm/1in) for making the seam.

In most cases, no specific instructions are given for finishing off inside seams. On clothing made from traditional Japanese fabric, the narrow width meant that long vertical seams were selvedges and garments were sized, to a degree, by taking wider or narrower turnings rather than being cut. Alternatively, garments such as kimono were lined. Seam finishing was therefore not a major consideration. Choose the method that best suits you, your project and your machine. Use an overlocker if you have one; zigzag seams either singly or together, depending on your pressing choices. Topstitch through top fabric and both turnings or finish with traditional western methods, such as felling or binding. The choice of method is more important when you are making a garment, such as a jacket, that you may take off in public, allowing the inside to be seen by others.

Your sewing will be more efficient if you can arrange to have pressing facilities near your machine. A travel iron can be convenient for small seams, where a full-size iron may crush another area undesirably, and is also lighter to lift if you want the iron at your side so you can press without leaving your seat. Test your fabrics before you begin stitching, to see whether you want or need to use steam, if available, or a press cloth. Your iron manual should indicate which temperature range suits which type of fibre, and most irons have the common fibre groups marked on the dial. Do not ignore this advice and never attempt to work with an iron that has a faulty thermostat. You might ruin the fabric and the work already invested in the garment.

Always press a seam before sewing across it. Quite often, you need to press under turnings on pieces before attaching them to the garment. This is because it is easier to achieve a consistent pressed width on the flat piece of fabric before it has been assembled and because the prepared edge will be easier to finish. If using a steam iron, beware of a rush of scalding hot steam from the iron. Some stitchers find that rubber finger stalls (used for counting currency notes) are a good protection against this risk.

Occasionally, even proficient workers find it necessary to undo a bit of stitching. However annoying it might be, try not to start the task in a poor frame of mind! If you have already pressed the seam, take a moment to press it 'closed' again so that as you unpick you are not digging into the valley of the seam. Cut stitches about every fourth or fifth one down one side, then turn the work over and pull the back thread out whole. Aside from pulling out the short bits manually, a tip is to put a piece of sticky tape lightly over the seam to collect most of the bits. Don't leave the tape on the fabric for long.

Be encouraged by the knowledge that most of the garments in this book are very simple to sew. They do not have very many pattern pieces or intricate details, nor do they demand lots of extra supplies or notions. Aside from time spent on decoration that you may choose to add, most can be machine-sewn in half a day, with perhaps a little hand finishing for the following evening.

# CHAPTER 1
# A Japanese approach to design

Whatever western style or period of design you prefer, you will be able to find some equivalent in Japan's design history that might be used as a source of inspiration. However, in the west we probably tend to think of Japanese design as minimalist, stylized and refined. One way to achieve a Japanese flavour to your garments, therefore, is to keep the design elements simple. A single motif on the centre back of a kimono, hanten or waistcoat is a design classic that is easy to copy, using whatever decorative technique you wish, and guarantees success. But what might that motif be and what if you want to do rather more?

## Kamon and marumon

These two words are often confused. A kamon is a Japanese family crest, the equivalent to a heraldic shield in Europe. In the past, noble families chose their crests, modifying them for various family members, and the laws governing the wearing of kamon were strictly enforced. At the end of World War II, the whole system of wearing crests was abolished and these attractive designs became public property. They still feature widely in daily life, as company logos, for example, and decorating a wide variety of objects. They are characterized by a stylized simplicity – a kind of condensation of the object in question.

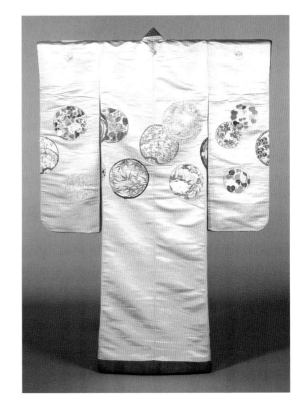

A marumon is any motif or group of motifs contained within a circle, either actual or imaginary. The circular shape is particularly pleasing to the eye and so was widely used for kamon. However, not all kamon are round: the diamond is another favoured shape. Equally, one can compose, for one's own use, a group of forms within a circular shape, and this would be a marumon but not a kamon. An example of this is the snowdrop marumon on the navy-and-white kimono (pages 22 and 27), which employs a popular arrangement of the flower form, repeated three times within the shape of a circle.

A good source of kamon designs is *Japanese Design Motifs*, by Fumi Adachi. With over 4,000 examples, you will not run short of inspiration. Many are simple enough to redraw, or you can photocopy and enlarge a few for a project in hand, as this is permitted by the publisher.

*Right* The exquisitely embroidered marumon arranged across the centre of this 19th-century kimono suggest it was worn without an obi as an open robe.

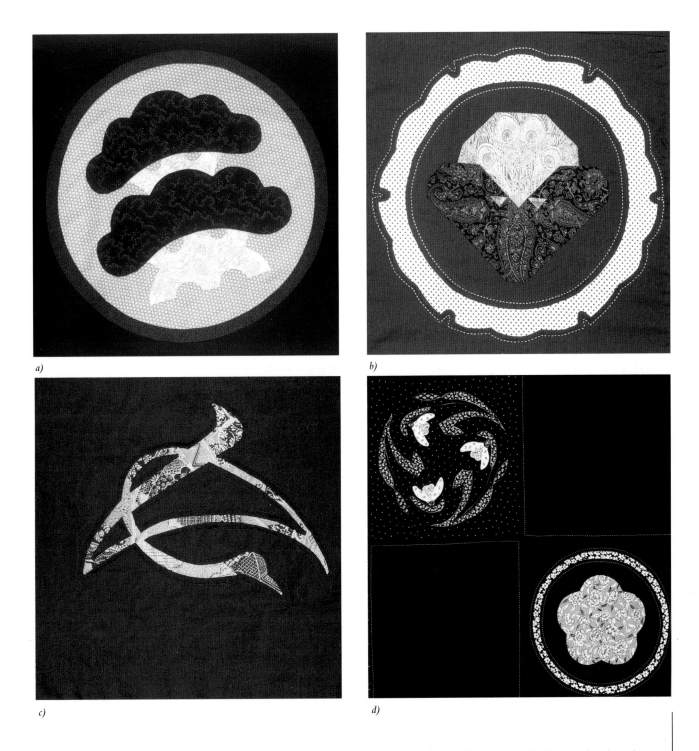

*a)* Centred on the upper back of a man's kimono, a single kamon adds an accent of colour to a low-key scheme.

*b)* An alternative to traditional appliqué, this pieced pansy, created by 1930s designer Ruby McKim, is applied in the centre of a fabric ring.

*c)* This calligraphic crane came from *Japanese Design Motifs*. See bibliography, page 126.

*d)* The snowdrop block (above left) features rotational symmetry and is described further opposite.

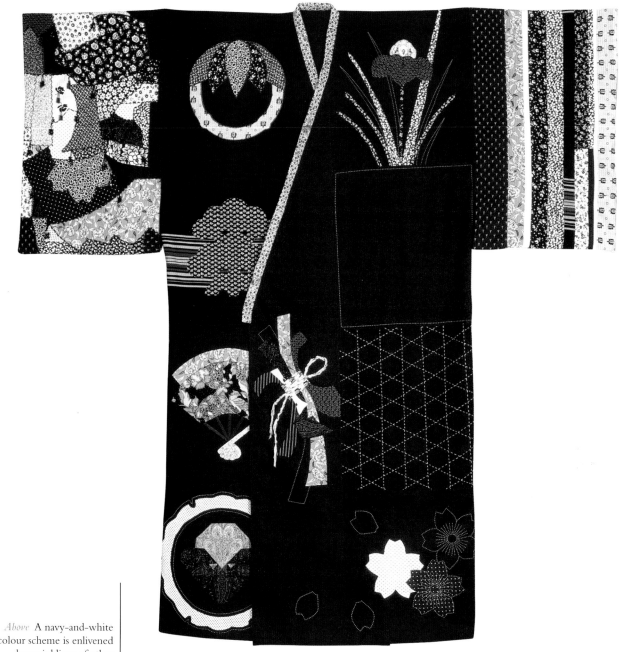

*Above*  A navy-and-white colour scheme is enlivened by sprinklings of other colours. The motifs include a *noshi* on the front extension for good fortune.

# Colour

It is impossible to write about design without mentioning colour, since the choice of colours affects how well a design works. Having lived in Japan for a number of years, a friend observed that the Japanese have a very different way with colour but that she still couldn't define what it was exactly. Nevertheless, here are a few ideas.

Firstly, indigo – or the family of blue shades that it can provide – is widely associated with every country of the Orient. It was the universal colour for the workaday clothes of ordinary people, even reaching higher levels in society through intricately dyed shibori textiles. It is not surprising that lots of beginners choose navy and white for a first kimono. It will be sure to work well, especially if you follow what appears to be a very Japanese trait – interpret the choice loosely! When collecting fabrics, especially prints, don't reject those that have the odd splash of other colours, particularly clear, bright hues. It is surprising how they enliven the overall appearance of the garment without destroying the perception that it is a navy/white colour scheme.

A good accompaniment for the navy-and-white partnership, naturally, is red. This classic combination has been around in the west for ages so it isn't surprising that many people feel comfortable with it. Red is considered to be a felicitous colour in the Orient as a whole. Consequently, in Japan, wedding kimono ensembles often feature quite a lot of red. Red comes in many forms, but the most popular is probably the scarlet/vermilion hue, in other words the orange end of red, rather than the crimson shades from the purple end. In particular, many Japanese fabrics printed to make girls' kimono seem to feature this colour.

Immediately you study kimono you realize that the Japanese have as full a colour palette as one could wish for. This is not surprising, considering that the Japanese are skilled master dyers. What can be unexpected is the colours they choose to put together. It may be instructive to search for a good illustration of a kimono, or find one in a museum, and list the colours it contains. Trying this exercise on the vintage kimono that I reassembled produces the following list:

a) background – putty (or warm grey);

b) background dyed pools of colour – purple, rust, white and cabbage green;

*Left Noshi* were gifts to the gods of dried abalone strips and often appear on wedding kimono as colourful slices of pattern.

c) motifs – deep purple, rust, vermilion, leaf green, holly green, mushroom, light yellow, shaded light blue, shaded pink/lilac;

d) plus embroidery in baby pink, mid blue, vermilion, silver and gold.

What rules might be operating here? At first sight, it might seem the answer is 'none'. However, further thought shows that the background is neutral – useful rule no. 1.

The background pools of colour are, with the exception of white (a neutral), secondary colours produced by mixing two of the primary colours together. Although these are used in quite saturated, full-strength forms, they are less eye-catching than primary colours would be, so they still read as background. This rule might be 'don't let the background compete'.

The motifs are worked in colours that are visually more eye-catching than the background: vermilion because it's bright and clear; deep purple because it's strong and dark, and the pastel shades also work for the opposite reason – because they're light. So the rule is 'use your brightest, strongest or most eye-catching colours for the most important elements in the design'. Not new, but still a useful reminder.

The three greens of the motifs are a mix that one would rarely find used together in the west. We tend to put colours into families: the 'blue' greens, the 'yellow' greens, even the 'brown' greens or 'grey' greens. Then we think that, in order to succeed, the colour scheme should keep to one family, having just shades of, say, 'blue' greens. What the Japanese seem to do is combine the different families. The approach works well, which is hardly surprising, for this is often what can be seen in nature.

*Above* This colourful scheme suggests the garment was for a young unmarried woman. Details such as filling in patterns in some colour pools provide visual rewards.

This is the final suggestion, best being described as 'going for the off-match'. Whereas in the west, we might search for 'just the right shade of ...', it seems to me that the Japanese eye favours a shade or tone which, if it is a purple in question, for example, has just a touch more red in it, or a bit more blue, and seeks that out deliberately, rather than considering it to be a second-best option.

Having decided to decorate your kimono with kamon executed in your chosen colour scheme, the next consideration is likely to be 'How to place them?' It seems to me, after some years of teaching, that maintaining a Japanese quality is the hardest thing for westerners to achieve. Even if you understand some of the differences between the design approaches, it can be hard to change what one does or finds pleasing.

# Odd numbers and asymmetry

These two concepts have been put under one heading because they are connected and both are characteristic of Japanese style. In the west, people often use and expect to see balanced arrangements with even numbers of motifs, all the same size, placed in identical positions at each side of an imaginary centre. Such formal symmetry is thought to appeal because it represents stability and harmony. It is relatively easy to achieve and, occasionally, predictable to the point of being dull.

In Japanese design, one is more likely to find an odd number of motifs, often five or seven, probably of mixed sizes, arranged in an asymmetrical way or scattered, apparently at random. Motifs may partly obscure one another or slip off the edge of a garment panel, as if they are floating freely instead of nailed in place. Balance and harmony are still important, but attained in different ways: perhaps a group of small elements here, counterbalanced by a single larger form there.

So the lesson is deliberately to avoid putting two motifs in exactly the same position – for example, one on each sleeve. Instead have one visible on the front and the other on the back, but maybe cut off at the wrist. Try spreading out your garment panels on the floor, in the sequence in which they will be sewn together, and scattering your motif patterns over the pieces. See where they fall; if you don't like it, try again. Alternatively, photograph your fabric on the computer and experiment with design possibilities.

*Left* This 16th-century kimono illustrates asymmetric design effectively through the use of a single large motif, here of bamboo. Note also the three kamon across the shoulders.

*Above* A kimono-shaped template was created on the computer then filled with photographed fabric to try several design ideas.

# Symbolism, seasons and motifs

Symbolism is deeply rooted in the Japanese mindset. An example is the Japanese businessman who, in the morning, looks out over a pocket handkerchief of a garden (Japan is a relatively small country and roughly one-sixth of it is uninhabitable, so building land is at a premium). The tiny garden has raked gravel, perhaps three interesting rocks and a modest bamboo – but what he sees symbolizes the sea or a river, the mountains and the forests.

A motif might exist because a samurai family chose that flower or plant as their crest – let us say, the plum blossom. Even though the form you see is stylized – in other words, it is not inhibited by too great a need for natural representation – it is almost always shown without leaves, because in nature the plum bears flowers before the leaves appear. Unlike the cherry, the flowers are not destroyed by a night or so of frost. By extension, therefore, the plum has come to symbolize more than just the season of winter; it also represents what today would be called staying power or constancy. Plum blossom can survive the hardship of winter and so one who wore it could feel also himself to be a survivor. Similar properties attach to the bamboo, also hardy, and the pine tree, so these three have come to be known as 'the three companions of the deep cold'. It is not surprising that they are among the most popular plants to be represented.

The Japanese love affair with nature and the seasons probably began at about the same time that the kimono developed as the national form of dress. Clothing used to be carefully colour-coded for the season, and as well as observing laws concerning social class, the motifs painted on a kimono would indicate for which season it was intended. It is not unusual to find motifs pertaining to two seasons: looking forward to the approaching change of season and also extending the time for which a garment could be worn (useful for those without a bottomless purse). For example, fans, representing summer, might mingle with chrysanthemums and maples for autumn, which is another significant season, and not just for the stunning colours offered by maple leaves. Autumn represents the ephemeral nature of life, as depicted by grasses, foliage and symbolic colours (one colour scheme was called 'barren fields'), all indicating inevitable decay.

So what might the western maker take from this storehouse of design? Firstly, there is clearly so much more than this brief essay can present. At the very least, perhaps one result might be a motivation to discover more. Hopefully, however, this has perhaps lifted a corner of a curtain, revealing the Japanese attitude to design and its values. My navy-and-white kimono was themed around winter because I have a January birthday, and on it I have a plum block, a pine tree and a bamboo ring. Perhaps the Japanese didn't know the snowdrop at the time kamon were developing so, after looking for one, I designed the marumon mentioned earlier. As I expected to wear the kimono all year round, I added irises for spring, fans and water for summer, and a crane for good fortune.

It is for each maker to find something within the symbolism that has personal meaning and so to draw on this inner creative spring with respect.

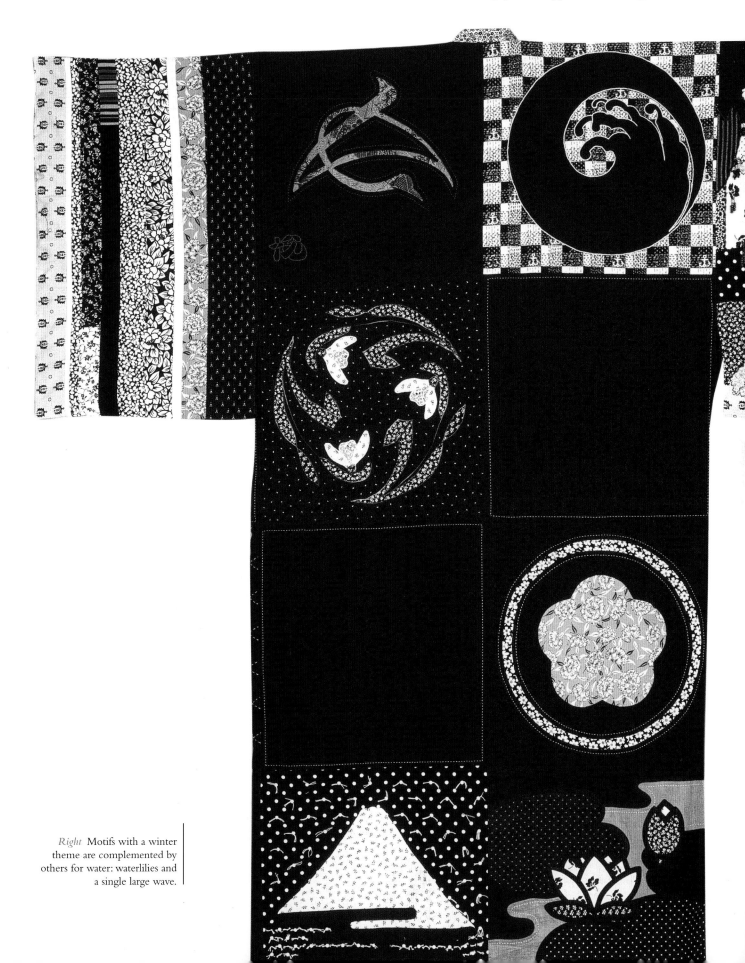

*Right* Motifs with a winter theme are complemented by others for water: waterlilies and a single large wave.

# CHAPTER 2
# Decorative techniques

This chapter covers some techniques that have been featured on the garments illustrated, at a level intended to get you started. Space does not permit exhaustive coverage of all the possibilities offered by these creative crafts, so our advice is always to seek out books or classes on specific techniques that you wish to master.

## Appliqué

This very popular decorative technique is well suited to the garments featured here. The navy-and-white kimono was initially made as a sampler to illustrate many techniques, but here we concentrate on two forms of appliqué: the first sewn by hand and the second using the machine.

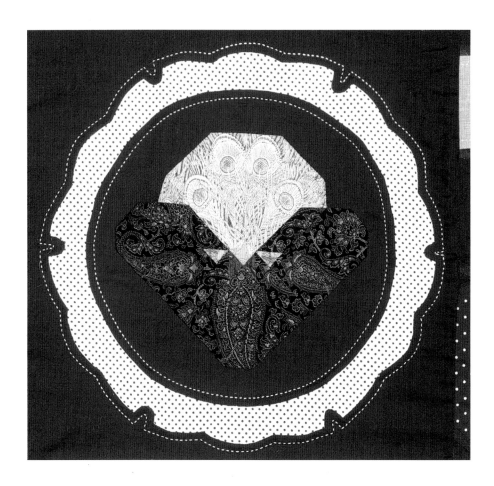

*Left* This pretty enclosure, called a snow ring, was inspired by the way snow melts away around plants.

# How to draft and appliqué fabric rings

The following instructions, which show how to centre a circle of one fabric over another accurately, leaving an outer ring of one fabric and an inner circle of the second (underlying) fabric, are ideal for kamon and marumon, as described in the previous chapter.

**1**   Cut a square of card large enough to accommodate the desired size of circle. Mark the centre of each side and join to form a cross.

**2**   Put the point of your compasses on the junction and draw both inner and outer rims of the size of circle you want. Larger circles look better if the space between the inner and outer lines is bolder than the space allowed for small ones.

**3**   Cut out accurately and smoothly to make a ring template, ensuring that the vertical and horizontal lines are visible crossing the template. This will help you to centre the template on the fabric at the next step.

**4**   Cut two squares of fabric, each at least 2.5cm (1in) larger than the finished motif required. One is the background and one is for the appliqué circle rim. At the simplest decorative level, the background could be just a pretty piece of fabric, perhaps featuring a printed flower. A Japanese interpretation would not centre the flower within the circle but instead position it slightly to one side.

**5**   With right side up, fold each fabric square in half and finger press the fold. Unfold, then fold in half the other way and finger press.

**6**   Place the card circle template on the right side of the fabric that is to be the ring, centring it by aligning the lines on the card with the vertical and horizontal folds on the fabric. Using a silver dressmaker's pencil or similar marker, draw around the template, both inside and outside, to mark both sewing lines.

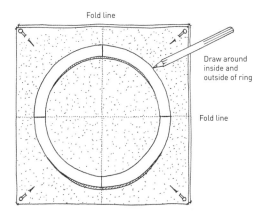

Fold line

Draw around inside and outside of ring

Fold line

**7**   Place this marked fabric right side up over the right side of the background fabric square; the folds on both squares should allow them to 'nest' together snugly. Pin, and then add a line of tacking (basting) neatly between the two marked rims.

**8**   Apply the inner rim first. Begin by making a small hole in the top layer of fabric only, cutting away the centre to leave a scant 7mm (¼in) allowance around the marked line for needle-turning neatly in place. After completing the inner rim, decide where on the garment the motif will be positioned. Trim excess background just within the rim, then attach the outer edge to the garment panel in a similar way.

Sew inner edge to background fabric.
This background fabric may be trimmed
so the outer edge could be sewn to a
garment panel

**9**   If you have a motif to place in the centre of the fabric ring, you might not wish to sew all around the inner rim initially but to leave a gap in the stitching where stems or leaves could be tucked under the rim. After the central motif is worked, complete attaching the inner rim before sewing the outer one.

# Bonded or fused appliqué

Used for the orange carp on the turquoise kimono, this method produces consistent results and, when executed carefully, is sufficiently durable to be used for clothing. A fusible web product, such as Bondaweb (Wonder Under) or HeatnBond, is used to attach the appliqué shape. The web is a fine mesh of heat-activated glue, mounted on a paper backing. Some products are intended for use without sewing, so be sure to buy a sewable version.

*Right* Here is the kimono made from the computer design on page 25.

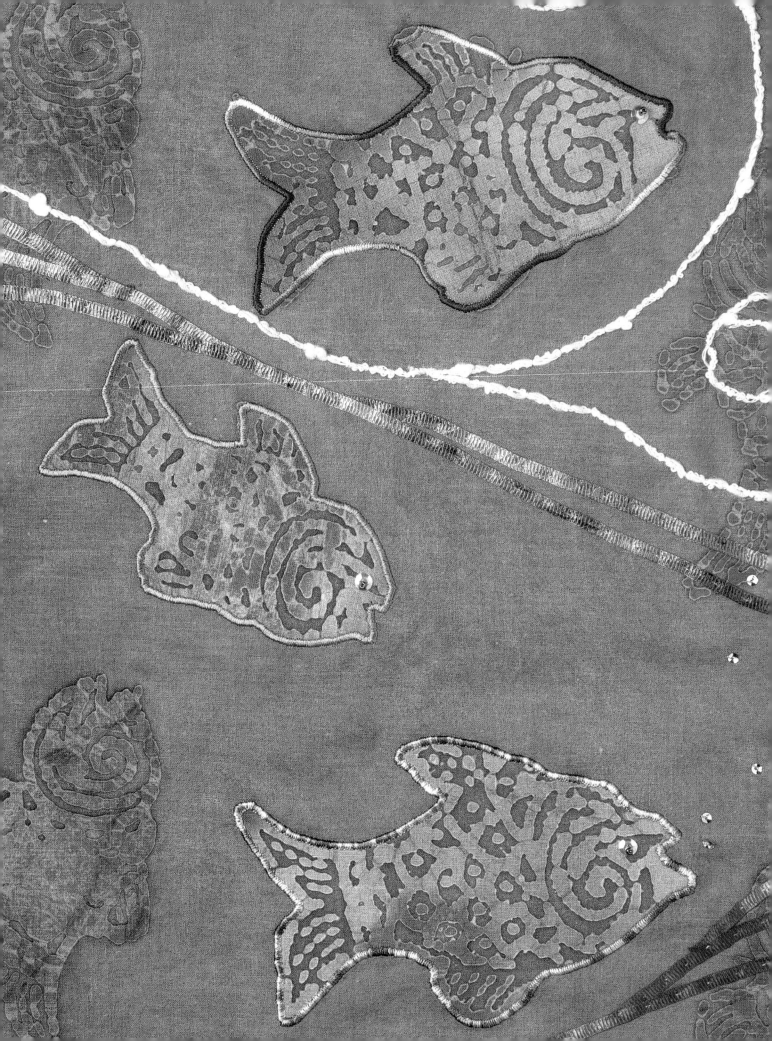

*Left* Batik carp fabric in two colourways prompted the use of orange fish from one applied to the lower-key blue version. Yarn and space-dyed tape suggest water and sequins become eyes and air bubbles.

**1** Choose the design that you want to make, such as the snowdrop marumon. As you are placing the fusible web on the back of the individual pieces to attach them to your background fabric, you need reverse images. The simplest method is to turn your original master pattern over and retrace the entire design on the back.

**2** If you now trace the component parts of the motif on the paper side of the fusible web, things should be correct. With paper-cutting scissors, cut out the traced shapes, leaving a small extra margin all around each. Fusible web can also be cut to match desired printed motifs, such as the carp, again leaving a small margin around the outer edge.

**3** Choose your fabrics and press them. Next, following the manufacturer's directions, fuse the web motifs to the wrong side of your fabrics. Allow the pieces to cool before handling, as the bond is not complete until cool.

**4** Cut out, following the drawn outlines or shapes of printed motifs but retaining the paper backing. Arrange the shapes on your background fabric, following the master pattern.

**5** When everything is correct, work around the design, peeling off the paper backing and returning each element to its position. A firm press with a warm hand will help keep the pieces in place until all are ready. Follow the maker's instructions to fuse all in position.

**6** The final step is to work around each part of the design with a zigzag or satin stitch on the sewing machine. Make a test before starting on the motif for your garment, using a single flower or leaf on a spare piece of the intended fabric. Find the correct tension (generally a little less than for straight sewing) and a pleasing stitch width and density, checking how closely the stitches should be packed together for the desired effect. Adjust this on the stitch length control. The wide range of machine embroidery threads available today means that you can enhance the design tremendously by your choice of thread. On the snowdrop example, the petals are sewn with plain white thread but the rest is worked in a shaded deep blue that adds a subtle extra dimension. It was also used to add the stems, which were too narrow to be made from fabric. The carp are worked with plain, shaded, variegated and metallic threads.

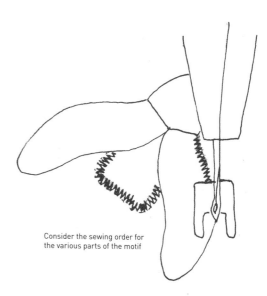

Consider the sewing order for the various parts of the motif

# Piecing or patchwork

Patchwork techniques existed in the East centuries ago, so are an obvious choice of method. These instructions use the hanten (Chapter 7) as an example but can be adapted for any of the garments. You can piece in many different arrangements, including traditional block designs.

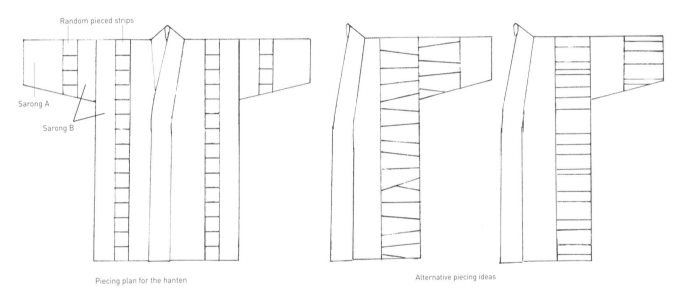

Piecing plan for the hanten                     Alternative piecing ideas

1   Cut a foundation panel for each part of the garment to be decorated. For the hanten, this would be the body and sleeve pieces. You might choose just to add some piecing, say, to the sleeves only. What matters is that you think of the garment as a whole when designing.

2   Press the panels well because any remaining wrinkles may prevent the work from lying flat. Decide which is the right side of the fabric, to be visible as lining inside the garment, and lay the panels wrong side up to receive the decoration.

3   Each patchwork panel is a strip that will have a finished width of 5cm (2in), pieced from smaller strips and squares. For easy calculation, a 1cm (⅜in) seam allowance was chosen, meaning pieces would need to be cut 7cm (2¾in) square in theory. In order to have matching pieced decoration on both fronts, however, it was decided to work double-width units, which could be cut lengthways in two, one for each pair of panels. The patches were therefore cut 7cm x 14.5cm (2¾ x 5¾in); the extra 5mm (¼in) is a safety margin to allow for trimming in case the edges of the pieced strip are uneven.

4   Cut a number of patches to this size, using a rotary cutter and mat if you have one. Try to include a few patches cut from the main (here, sarong) fabrics to unify the pieced strips with the neighbouring areas. In order to have a suitably random look, sort the patches into piles for the various panels, ensuring that the fabrics are evenly shared around the units. Calculate the approximate number of patches needed, then arrange them into sequences.

Work two sets in tandem

**5** When sewing, work with two piles at a time but be careful not to mix them up. Place the first two patches from pile A, with right sides together, and sew, taking a 1cm (⅜in) seam allowance. Leave this pair in the machine and do the same with the first two from pile B. Now cut the pile A pair from the machine and add the third patch to this pair. Repeat for the pile B set. Continue in this way until all patches are joined and you have two units of equal length. Press the seams open for the best finished appearance. Lay the units out to check that they will be the length required for the panel. If not, cut and add patches as required and press again. Now measure and cut the pieced strips lengthways to produce 7cm (2¾in) strips, trimming as necessary.

**6** To discover where to position the pieced strip on the foundation, check the size of the first sarong strip to be used. Remember that 1cm (⅜in) seam allowance will be used by joining the edge of the strip and likewise, the same amount will be used on the pieced strip. Therefore the positioning line for the strip needs to be 2cm (¾in) nearer the edge of the foundation than the width of the strip. Draw a line and place the strip, right side up, as straight as possible. Pin and tack (baste) in position, as on next page. Next place the sarong strip on top, right side down with raw edges level. Pin and sew, choosing a thread to match the foundation as this will be visible inside the garment. Press the sarong strip towards the edge of the foundation. Repeat to add the second sarong strip on the other side of the pieced unit.

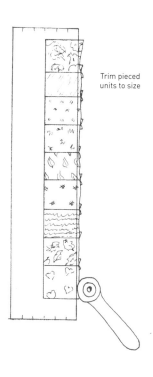

Trim pieced units to size

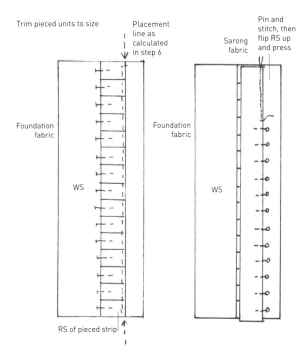

7   When working the back panel, although you still need two pieced units, the centre back panel will probably be cut on a fold. To achieve the same appearance, with the seam allowances lying under the sarong strips, modify the method by sewing the pieced strips, one each side of the main fabric centre panel, before joining all to the foundation. Press. Centre this unit over the foundation and add a line of machining 'in the ditch' between panel and pieced strip on each side. Then add the outer sarong strips just as before.

*Right* Strip patchwork is easy yet provides pattern and colour.
Including a few patches of main fabrics unites the whole.

# Sashiko

Enthusiasts of Japanese textiles will doubtless already know that this name refers to the stitched patterns, worked in white thread upon indigo-dyed fabric, that were often used to strengthen and decorate the jackets of workers such as fire-fighters and farmers. The bold designs in white sometimes announced to which village or lord the workers belonged and, no doubt, helped to make the men visible in the smoke of a fire.

In the west, perhaps we focus too readily upon the decorative aspect of sashiko, for several of the traditional garments studied for this book show sashiko worked, not in white, but in dark navy thread. The stitching can scarcely be seen, so the decorative effect is slight, but if you hold the garment in your hand you can feel the texture of the stitching and the body it imparts to the cloth.

There are many excellent books available on sashiko, and these are a good source for the geometric patterns strongly associated with the technique. However, to begin one needs only thread, a needle and a motif of choice.

Mark the design on the chosen fabric, using your preferred method (see pages 16–17). If you are stitching through more than one layer of cloth, tack (baste) the layers together.

## Thread

Authentic sashiko thread is now available in the west but other types will work satisfactorily. Try fine (no. 40 or 60) crochet cotton which, with its mercerized high-twist appearance, has an attractive texture. Alternatively, use cotton perlé, which is not as twisted or shiny, but still pleasing, or silk twist – more expensive but very classy. To experiment with what you have already, look for a fairly bold thread with some twist (if there is no twist, you will find your thread shreds too readily to work very far).

*Left* A late 19th-century garment combines three sashiko designs of varying scale and density.

# Needles

Choose a needle with an eye to accommodate the thread chosen. It needs to make a hole large enough for the thread to pass through without difficulty. The needle is therefore likely to be quite large, so you might try the Japanese manner of working a number of stitches onto the needle before pushing them all off – efficient if you can master it!

Begin with a knot on the back of the work and come through to the front. Sashiko stitches are larger than western quilting, but the actual size should look right for the thread and fabric chosen. Loosely woven fabrics demand bigger stitches. Quite a few books suggest the space should be about half the stitch size, but on most authentic Japanese examples I have seen, the stitches and spaces are about equal in length. Do not over-tighten the stitching: you are not attempting to create the plump or dimpled surface of western quilting.

Work the design in the most efficient sequence. With all-over geometric patterns, the traditional method is to work all lines in a particular direction first, then all in another direction, and so on, leaving any isolated fillings to be worked last. Japanese sashiko books often number the lines of a pattern for the best working sequence, as shown here. Buying sashiko thread in a skein, one can cut the skein so that all threads are equal in length, then all joins in the same part of the pattern fall at the same place. One can see this approach inside the longer hanten, which has a neat row of knots across the back. As they are a consequence of the way in which the stitching is worked, these knots have a right to be there so do not offend the Japanese eye.

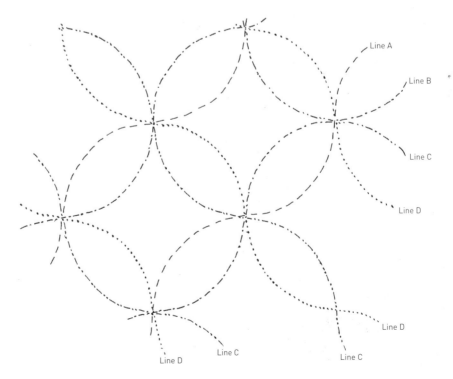

# Shibori

Shibori is a Japanese collective name for various ways of resist-dyeing cloth. It developed to decorate fabric at a time when sumptuary laws prohibited the wearing of luxury woven fabrics by anyone other than nobility. At first a less expensive method, as designs grew in complexity the labour-intensive process meant that shibori fabrics eventually rivalled brocades in extravagance. The technique became a speciality of the area around the town of Arimatsu, where whole families would spend the winter preparing cloth to be dyed outdoors in the summer. Today, little genuine shibori is produced in Japan (what there is comes from countries such as Korea), but its distinctive appearance is copied in both printed and woven textiles and has been widely adopted by textile artists.

Other cultures also use similar methods, basically all 'low-tech' and suited to simple designs and patterns. The dyeing technique is very accessible to beginners yet holds plenty of promise for creative development. Shibori involves shaping the cloth by some means. The following notes focus on stitching. An element of the unexpected – also called serendipity – is common to many shibori processes. Enough background – let's get on to the tools and process.

*Left* Experienced craftsmen
work intricate shibori designs
like this purely by eye.

## Needles

These must be sharp and have an eye large enough to carry the thread you choose. As the traditional method of working some patterns resembles sashiko, where you manipulate many stitches onto the needle before drawing the thread through them all, it makes sense to have a long needle, such as a 'straw'. Sometimes you must choose the needle to suit the fabric: many folds require a strong needle to push through multiple layers, while fine fabrics may be damaged by the same needle. Basic advice is to use a needle appropriate to the fabric and the pattern you plan to work.

## Thread

This must be strong enough to withstand being gathered tightly. I have successfully used pre-waxed quilting thread, which is very strong. For machine samples, I used monofilament quilting thread on top and machine sewing thread on the bobbin. This combination also resisted the dye effectively.

It can be interesting to experiment with different threads. As a general rule, the thicker the thread, the bolder the line it makes.

*Left* A vintage red silk sits beside ironed hand-dyed cotton lining: their distinctive crinkles announce that both are genuine shibori.

# Fabric

Pre-wash all fabric to remove any dressing or special finishes, unless a particular fabric has been sold as 'prepared for dyeing'. The suggested dyes work best on pure cotton, so if you accidentally use a piece of polycotton you will notice a conspicuous difference in the depth of colour: the more polyester content there is, the paler the colour will be. Washed unbleached calico is a useful basic fabric, but differences in saturation of colour may appear. If you don't want a white line on a coloured ground, then it is equally easy to get a coloured line on a darker ground by choosing a plain-coloured cotton. The resisted areas remain the original colour, while the rest is dyed. Expect the original colour to affect the appearance of the new dye colour, too.

# The stitches

It is most helpful to make stitch experiments for yourself. To test stitches, just work straight lines or diagonals, lightly marked with a finger-crease before sewing. Below are some possibilities.

1  Simple running stitch on single cloth, hira-nui, or running stitch close to the edge of a fold of fabric, ori-nui. Another option, maki-nui, is to oversew along a fold of fabric, using a winding action, as shown, to take the needle over the folded edge and insert it back towards you. If you prefer to use the sewing machine, use the longest stitch setting on a single layer of cloth and the same threads and setting on a double layer of cloth.

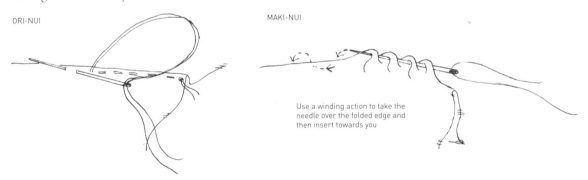

ORI-NUI

MAKI-NUI

Use a winding action to take the needle over the folded edge and then insert towards you

2  For hand-sewn samples, generally use a double thread with a large knot, close to but not right at the end. Double thread is the easiest to secure at the end as the two threads can be tied several times into a chunky knot that will not pull out. It is also less likely to break during gathering. Experiment, however, with lines stitched with single and double thread. A single thread generally makes a finer resisted line and so it may be worth taking the chance of the thread breaking. Two single threads from separate but nearby lines can be knotted together after they have been drawn up tightly. Sewing through two layers of cloth also generally produces a bolder line on both layers.

**3** For the most part, aim to keep your stitches even. However, the resulting pattern is influenced by the size of stitch you make. Deliberately changing the size of stitch partway along a line of the design (or on neighbouring lines) will change its appearance.

**4** Sashiko quilting grid designs are also very useful for making shibori fabrics. Avoid marking the design with pencil as this is difficult to remove once the gathers are in place. Either lightly crease a grid, then sew the desired pattern on the grid, or trace the design using a wash-away marker. After sewing the motif but before gathering up the design, wash away the marked line and dry the cloth. I learned how important this is when I forgot to do so on a sample and found the marker line clearly visible and fixed after dyeing, but now a different shade!

**Sew all of the design before beginning to gather up any of it.**

# Gathering the stitched pattern

**1** After sewing all the pattern, gather the fabric along the threads. Compress the cloth as closely as possible and knot the threads to keep the cloth compressed during dyeing.

**2** Large areas or complex designs are best gathered a little at a time along all lines, then a little more along all lines and so on. This makes it easier to see that all lines of the pattern are gathered, besides being physically easier to do. If you gather one thread to its limit, this can create such volume to the cloth that a neighbouring line can be difficult to gather fully.

**3** This method also makes it easier to replace a thread, if necessary. If a thread breaks when the nearby threads are fully tightened, they may have to be eased loose again in order to resew a line of the pattern.

**4** Threads may break while being gathered, but a more common problem is to find that the beginning knot has pulled out. If this happens, it is not necessary to replace the whole thread. Instead, ease the cloth along the thread until you can rethread it into your needle. Rework the stitches, if possible in the same holes, and knot the ends again (better!).

**5** Gather long threads from both ends. Having the beginning knot a little away from the very end of the thread makes it easier to find this tail and pull on it. When gathered as tightly as possible, there will be plenty of thread, allowing the first knot to be cut off and the two threads tied together.

**6** Be methodical as you gather up and secure a pattern. On some designs it is easy to omit knotting some gathered threads. These may remain sufficiently tight to give you a pattern or they may work loose during the dyeing process, producing a softer version than intended.

## Stitching motifs

**1**  Besides stitching all-over patterns, you can make shibori motifs. For example, you could stitch versions of motifs inspired by fabrics purchased for a project. Or you could choose motifs found in books on Japanese or other forms of design.

**2**  Lightly mark the motif on the washed and ironed cloth. Any type of stitching can be used to sew a motif. Two different stitching methods in the same motif can give an interesting change of pattern.

**3**  Often the motif appears as a light outline around a shape coloured the same as the ground. To resist the inside of the motif as well requires an extra step. Stitch, gather and knot as usual. Coax the resulting clump of fabric into a neat form and bind with more thread. Leave a good tail at the beginning for returning to tie off after binding. If the binding threads are wound very closely next to each other they create a very solid resist. Winding in a very open way, up towards the tip and criss-crossing back, will permit more dye to create interesting patterns inside the shape.

Stitch motif and gather tightly

Bind the enclosed motif bundle

## Capping

This is another way to resist the whole of your chosen motif. Place something that will resist the dye on one side of the cloth then sew the shape through both the resist and the cloth. In the example shown here, a double layer of clingfilm (saran wrap) was carefully stitched to one side of the fabric. Gather up the shape very tightly, with the resist layer outwards so that there is scarcely any passage through the gathered 'navel'. Although the resist is only on one side of the fabric, the air trapped within prevents dye getting to the other side of the cloth and therefore the resist is effective. Used double, clingfilm makes a good resist! It is readily available and though it clings to the needle a bit whilst sewing it is relatively easy to stitch.

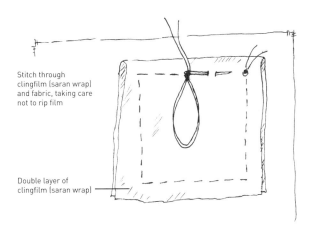

Stitch through clingfilm (saran wrap) and fabric, taking care not to rip film

Double layer of clingfilm (saran wrap)

# Dye

Use fibre-reactive dyes, such as Procion. If you don't have these, the most widely available fibre-reactive dyes are Dylon Cold Water dyes. Available in pots, the latter are intended to dye about 175–225g (6–8oz) of cloth to the shade illustrated. Weigh your stitched samples before dyeing to be sure you have enough dye for the samples prepared. If you put too much cloth into the dye-bath, the resulting colour will be paler. To make each pot of dye powder into a dye-bath, you also need salt and either a sachet of Dylon Cold Fix or washing soda crystals. Always follow the manufacturer's directions to make up a dye-bath.

## General dyeing advice

1  Most people don't have a separate room in which to dye, so they use either the bathroom or the kitchen because they have a readily available source of water. In the kitchen, be sure there is no uncovered food that could be contaminated by dye powder in the air. Wear a face mask if you wish. Contact-lens wearers can wear goggles to avoid airborne dye colouring plastic lenses.

2  Wear old clothes and shoes (in case of splashes or spills) and rubber gloves. Cover work surfaces (and floor if you are messy!) with newspaper or plastic sheeting.

3  Don't use containers or measuring jugs that you use for food. Use a plastic or metal bucket or other large container as a dye-bath. You also need an old teaspoon and tablespoon, and a stirrer. A length of clean garden cane makes a reasonable stirrer, but if you do much dyeing a plastic brewer's spoon is an ideal and not expensive tool. I also demoted some ageing kitchen tongs to my dyeing kit, but if you wear rubber gloves you can just lift out the dyed pieces with your hands.

4  A timer, or maybe two if you have two dye-baths, will also be useful.

5  Follow the product instructions for immersion dyeing. This is usually to stir continuously for about the first 10 minutes. After this, stir intermittently until a full hour has passed. Stirring regularly gives a more even colour. It will be easier to stir the fabric if you have a good depth of liquid. Topping up the dye-bath to a good depth won't reduce the colour achieved as long as the weight of fabric doesn't exceed the amount stated. Colour strength depends on the dye powder/cloth ratio, not the amount of water.

6  When the gathers are tightly formed, they may collect accumulations of dye, giving dark marks. As this is a consequence of the process, the Japanese would not be troubled by it. If you dislike this effect, however, you could reduce the chances of this happening by rearranging the folds of the cloth a little during the stirring. If you like the effect, keeping the cloth still will encourage patchy effects.

7  After dyeing, rinse the fabric until the water runs clear. Next, wash, rinse and dry. You can spin-dry the samples, if you want. If any resist stitching comes undone during the rinsing and washing stages, don't panic. The areas resisted while in the dye-bath will not be lost, due to dye present in the rinsing water. In some cases, the samples will dry better if the resist stitching is undone or loosened at this stage. However, it can be difficult to remove thread swollen with water from the wet cloth, so either way is fine.

8  Beware of skimping on this step. Inadequately rinsed and washed fabric can dye your clothes pegs, and you might acquire 'tidemarks' from fabric that has been hanging over the line or been sprayed to remove heavy creases. You might also stain your ironing board cover.

# Silk painting
## Supplies

Most places specializing in dye and craft products will sell ranges of silk paint products and the necessary accessories, such as brushes, frames and pins. Beginners are best advised to start with products that can be fixed by ironing.

You may find a local supplier for the silk or send for it by mail order. Silk fabrics come in various weights and widths, so check to see which width best suits your chosen pattern as well as the best weight for the style of garment.

You can use embroidery frames for silk dyeing, but these tend to be small and so may limit the scale at which work can be done. The hippari panel (right, and page 65, top) was pinned in a scarf frame, home-made from soft wood. Wrap wooden frames in strips of plastic to keep them clean.

*Right*  This design was laid out with gold gutta. The enclosed outlines were flooded with colour then details added last.

# Preparation

Pin your silk to the frame with Assa pins (three-pronged pins for use on delicate fabrics, available from craft shops), working from side to side, one at a time, and then from end to end until taut. Alternatively, insert the fabric as tightly as possible into an embroidery frame. Work over a plastic sheet and in good light. To avoid wasting paint, mix shades in small jam jars.

There are several methods of silk dyeing and each produces a slightly different effect from the others, so always make tests before advancing to the main project.

## Salt technique

Wet silk with clean water. Paint various colours onto the surface, then sprinkle with sea salt. Leave to dry. The salt can be reused several times. Leave the fabric overnight and then press, with the iron on the silk setting, to fix as directed (probably about three minutes). Wash the dyed fabric and roll it in a towel to blot away any excess, then iron while wet. If desired, you can work further into this with permanent marker pens and so on. You can also experiment with the salt method on dry silk.

## Gutta and pen outliners

On dry silk, doodle or trace closed designs, such as leaf outlines or freehand motifs copied from architecture. Keep them simple, avoiding tiny details. With a fine paintbrush, add a little silk paint into the centre of the motif and allow it to bleed to the outlined edge. Don't overload your brush: add a drop more at a time. Mix colours to see what effects you can achieve. Note that on warm days, paint dries quicker. When the colours have dried, iron-fix on the reverse side and then finish as directed above.

## Watercolour technique

Wet the silk and paint the colours on the background. Dry with a hairdryer. Add other details using outliners or denser paints. Try a dry-brush technique – dip a fine brush into paint, take off surplus with tissue and draw a fine line on the silk. Fine OHP pens also work well for fine detail. Again, finish as above.

## Cake-decorating pens

You can make your own silk paint pens by loading empty cake-decorating pens with silk paint. Dip a clean wick in the colour of your choice, insert into the barrel and off you go! Exhausted wicks can be reloaded, but only with the same colour or a deeper shade. These are controllable for line work such as writing.

Don't be afraid to experiment. Write down what you did in your design notebook, preferably with a sample alongside, in case you want to repeat the effect again.

# CHAPTER 3 Kimono

The kimono is a generic name for robes worn by both men and women. Having been around for over 1,000 years, these have experienced many changes in form. The following notes refer to the type of full-length garment given in the pattern below.

Traditionally made of narrow Japanese fabric (35cm/14in in width), the main body panels are cut in a single length from the back hem to run over the shoulder and down to the front hem. There is thus a centre back seam, but no shoulder seams. To provide enough fabric for the front overlap, a strip of fabric, called an extension, is added at the centre front edge of each main front panel. In wear, the left front is always worn over the right, for both men and women.

Sleeves are sewn to the outer edge of the body panels. Women's sleeves usually have an underarm opening, resulting from not sewing the sleeve to the body or the back to the front at the side seam immediately under the arm. The sleeve is cut from the standard width of fabric, so it does not reach right to the wrist. When the length of the sleeve is discussed, this refers to the amount of fabric hanging towards the garment hem. The pattern has sleeves of moderate length because I found them to be practical: sleeves that are very cropped are too short to be kept out of harm's way.

*Left* A 19th-century kimono dyed and embroidered with water and carp at the hemline, inspiration for our version, page 25.

*Right*  Note the flow of the design from sleeve to body, then body to sleeve, even though this would rarely be apparent in wear.

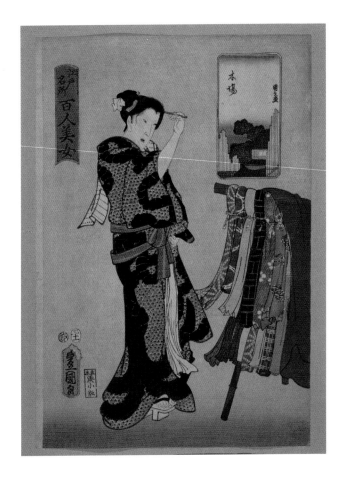

The kimono has a long collar, attached with a sloping seam across the front extension and into the front panel. A kimono has no fastenings, no pockets and requires some kind of tie around the waist to keep it in place, unless it is intended to be worn as an open robe. Women's kimono were traditionally longer than the shoulder-to-ankle length used for men. They had to be arranged into a fold over a cord tied around the waist, with the obi fastened on top.

Nearly everyone has heard of the obi (especially crossword fans!), but though a beautiful item of attire, it is not very practical. An obi is an elaborate, highly formalized tie consisting of several parts, including a broad, stiff sash that requires help in tying and is very restricting. It is never worn by men. In earlier times, the kimono could just be secured with a simple sash, and this is the mode recommended here. Though historical re-creation is not the purpose of this book, many women will be delighted to hear that a tightly cinched waist was not the desirable appearance when wearing a kimono. Instead, you should aim for a neat, cylindrical look, with the tie just firm enough to keep the wrap-over front in position. Most men's sashes are fairly narrow (approximately 7.5cm/3in), but long enough to wrap all around the body twice before being tied at the front with a bold knot, leaving short tails.

For practical purposes, for both men or women, the kimono below should be made to reach the feet or ankles. When sashed, it will then be just sufficiently above the ground for easy walking. You may save fabric by measuring the intended wearer and reducing the panel lengths if you wish. Alternatively, cut panels as directed and simply make a deeper hem.

Among a fascinating box of vintage kimono scraps, I found many that had signs of their construction still visible upon them. One feature common to them all was the general simplicity with which they had been made. They came from a period when kimono were hand sewn with a simple running stitch instead of sewn by machine. First-time makers, particularly those not familiar with western dressmaking techniques, should be encouraged by this simplicity of construction. Of course, if you are familiar with more advanced construction methods, you may apply them readily to making your kimono.

# Kimono ■ Materials and cutting notes

- 4.2m (4½yds) of fabric, 114cm (45in) wide
If you are buying kimono fabric, 1 tan is a standard kimono length.

For cutting layouts see pages 106–107.

- Seams may be eliminated to make best use of your fabric. Do not cut the collar until directed in the assembly instructions. The sash may then be cut from what remains.

## Assembling the unlined kimono

- The seam allowance is 1cm (⅜in) unless stated otherwise.

- RS = right side, WS = wrong side

The numbers below relate to the main assembly diagram for the kimono (fig A on page 52). Remember that, depending on how you decided to cut the kimono, not all steps will apply every time.

**1** In general, separate panels receive any decorative additions before they are assembled. Sometimes, however, motifs may need to be added after a specific construction step: for example, a motif intended to sit over the centre back seam cannot be applied until the seam is sewn. In this case, make supplementary notes to remind you to complete the task at the right time.

**2** Join centre back seam, with RS together and sewing as straight as you can.

**3** Remembering that you need a left and a right front, press a narrow double hem to the WS on the front edges of both extensions and tack (baste) in place. Attach the extensions to their respective fronts, at seams 3a and 3b on the diagram. Press these seams towards the sides and away from the centre. Mark the start of the front angles for the neckband on the RS of each front. For practical wear, this is best placed somewhere between one third and one half of the length of the front panel down from the shoulder. Make both the same.

**4** If you have used the alternative cutting plan, join fronts to backs at the shoulder-line, having the outer (side) edges level and leaving 4.5cm (1¾in) for a woman and up to 6.5cm (2½in) for a man each side of the centre back unstitched (fig B). If you cut the back and front as one length, cut this neck opening level with the shoulder-line.

**5** With a long straight-edge rule and a non-permanent marker, such as tailor's chalk, connect the start of the front angle to the neckline end of the shoulder seam on each front (fig C). Do not cut off excess fabric. Now measure the length of strip required for the collar, starting at one front edge up to the shoulder, continuing across the back neck and down the second front to the edge. The collar strip needs to be 5–10cm (2–4in) longer than this measurement to neaten the ends, so add this to decide the total length. Cut the collar this length by twice the desired width, plus 2cm (¾in). Divide the extra for finishing in half and mark on the collar to show where to begin attaching to the fronts. Next press a 1cm (⅜in) turning to the WS on one long edge of the collar to make finishing simpler. Sew the collar to the body in three steps, having its

**A**

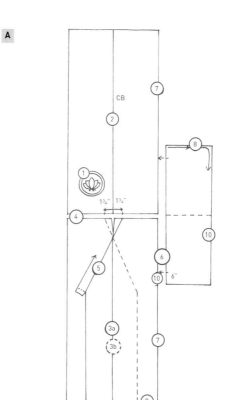

**B**

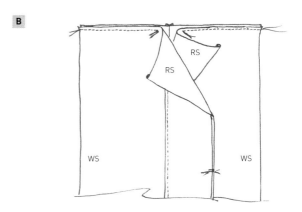

**C**

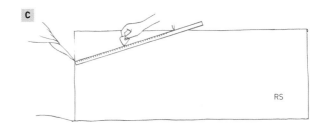

D

RS

WS

E

WS

RS

F

20cm
(8in)open

G

If choosing curved
corners on sleeves, run a
gathering thread across
the angle and draw up for
a smooth fit when RS out

long raw edge overlapping your drawn line by 1cm (³⁄₈in) as you pin into place. Begin sewing at the front edge up to the shoulder and leaving the shoulder seam allowance (if there is one) free (fig D). Remove from the machine and press. Then, folding the shoulder seam clear, bring the collar around to the back neck and pin into place as far as the second shoulder seam only. Stitch, keeping to an even 1cm (³⁄₈in) turning and leaving the shoulder seam free (fig E). Remove from the machine and press. Bring the collar round to the second front and pin, continuing to follow the drawn line to the front edge with the 1cm (³⁄₈in) seam allowance, then sew and press. Return to finishing the collar later.

**6** Fold one sleeve in half and match this midpoint to the shoulder seam on one side of the body. Repeat with the second sleeve. Stitch the sleeves to the body, leaving about 15cm (6in) at each end unstitched. Make a small bar tack, either by hand or on the machine, at each end of the seams for reinforcement.

**7** Fold the kimono in half across the shoulder-line and match the front and back hems. Starting about 15cm (6in) below where the sleeve seam ends, sew fronts and backs together at side seams (fig F). Reinforce the seams with a bar tack at the underarm end.

**8** Beginning at the sleeve underarm corner, sew the horizontal sleeve seam, if wished continuing round the corner and part way up the 'wrist' edge (fig F). (This corner may be curved.) Be sure to leave at least 20cm (8in) unstitched below the shoulder-line fold for the wrist opening. This makes the sleeve like a bag or pocket.

**9** Hem the lower edge, either by hand or machine, depending on your preference.

**10** Press in narrow turnings at openings, for example the underarms on body and sleeve, and wrist openings. Stitch as necessary, by hand or machine.

# Finishing the collar

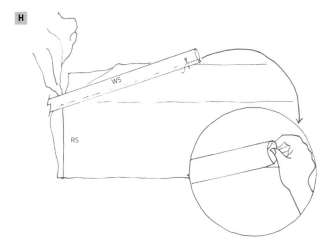

**11** Fold the collar in half, RS together, and bring the ends level at the two tails. On each front, sew the short seam to secure the ends of the collar. Turn RS out and tuck the extending tails back inside themselves until they are even with the front edge (fig H). Press the collar in what will be its finished size and position.

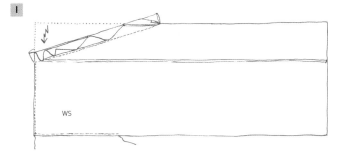

**12** Working on one front at a time, place the garment RS down on a large flat surface and now fold the excess front fabric above the collar in a concertina fashion parallel to the stitching, to fit within the depth of the pressed collar (fig I). This provides the equivalent of interfacing to give the front collar some additional body. Make sure each fold is very slightly within the previous one so that it will not be in the way when you stitch the turned edge of the collar in place to finish. When you are satisfied with the arrangement of folds, press and, if wished, tack (baste) in place. Repeat on the second front, then slip-stitch the remaining long edge of the collar to the stitching to attach it. Lastly, slip-stitch collar ends closed.

# Making a lined kimono

The main difference here is that attaching the collar becomes the last step. Start by assembling the outer fabric as above, up to and including step 8, but with the following differences:

at step 3, do not neaten the front edges;

at step 5, mark the collar positioning line and establish collar length only, but do not attach collar.

Next also make up the lining body (again no collar) as above as far as step 8, but do not attach the sleeve linings at step 6. Instead, simply sew on each sleeve separately, ensuring the wrist openings are the same size on both outer and lining.

To combine the outer and lining, slide the lining over the outer garment with RS together, having the raw edges level. Pin then sew the layers together from the marked collar attachment point down one front edge, turn the corner and continue along the hem to the second front, turning again to proceed up to the second collar attachment point (fig J). Slip the lining of one sleeve over one outer sleeve, RS together, and sew them together around the wrist opening only (fig K). Turn the sleeve lining to the inside of the sleeve through the wrist opening. Repeat with the second sleeve. Now turn the body lining to the inside of the garment and smooth into place, matching the shoulder and side seams and pressing the stitched outer edges.

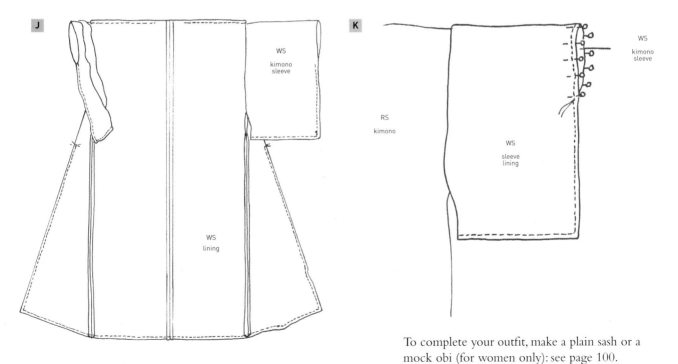

To complete your outfit, make a plain sash or a mock obi (for women only): see page 100.

Neaten at the sleeves by lapping the body lining over the sleeve lining with a small turning and slip-stitch into place. Also slip-stitch the lining to the outer fabric around the underarm openings.

With the lining fully settled in place, tack (baste) along the marked collar attachment line through both layers. Attach the collar, following the basic instructions at step 5 and proceeding straight to the instructions for finishing the collar to complete.

An alternative sleeve method on a lined garment leaves the whole wrist edge open. Sew only the short horizontal seam on both outer fabric and lining. With RS together, slip lining over the outer, sew together for the whole length of the long wrist edge seam, turn and press.

# Kimono for children

Kimono are not scaled down for children in the way that western clothing tends to be. For the most part, kimono-width cloth is used for the garment panels, but with a more generous seam allowance. To make the garment narrower over the shoulders, tucks are taken as described in the assembly instructions for the chan-chanko (see page 86). The size of the tucks varies, depending on the size of the child, and tucks can be changed as the child grows. Deep hems are common, allowing for letting down as the child grows.

The boy's kimono seen here has no front extensions, the collar being attached on a straight line down the front. It is worn over hakama (pleated trousers) as an open robe, tied in front, and is therefore lined. The kimono does, however, have underarm openings, like those of women's kimono, and there is a small tapered side panel included, as for the haori.

The sleeves also begin as full-width fabric, hemmed at the wrist end or faced, but with a seam allowance matching that on the side seams where they are attached to the body. Such extra fabric is always either caught in place by stitching or covered by lining, so the folds are not disturbed by being put on or taken off.

*Above* A boy's kimono in indigo-dyed yukata cotton shows an alternative sleeve shape and a colourful lining featuring motifs associated with boys.

# CHAPTER 4 Mompe

These traditional trousers, worn by men or women, usually finish above the ankle, probably to keep the bottoms from becoming wet and dirty during agricultural work! The pair shown here, from which the pattern has been derived, have a gusset to provide the extra width through the legs that would be lacking on traditional narrow Japanese cloth. The pattern has eliminated this gusset, assuming that western fabrics will be used. This also removes a seam that can rub the inside of the legs. Although basic mompe pre-date the invention of elastic, the version given here includes a waistline casing for elastic, as this is easy to sew besides being practical and comfortable to wear. The waistline casing could just as easily carry a drawstring threaded through a single channel instead of the twin channels stitched for the elastic.

*Left* The source of the pattern was this well-used pair, made from indigo-dyed cotton. The garment is timeless and practical.

*Above* Two versions of mompe: cotton lawn with elastic waist beside a longer silk pair with a drawstring.

Translating mompe into the western wardrobe, they most obviously become leisurewear: either the holiday outerwear variously called Capri pants or clam-diggers or, as featured above left, the bottoms of a pair of pyjamas, where the top is based on the hippari pattern. There is no reason to feel limited by the cropped length – make mompe the length you prefer. A full-length pair, worn under a tunic or wrap-over top or jacket, will make a dressier ensemble for more formal events, yet still maintains the original ease of construction and comfort in wear. A silk pair, above right, accompany the haori made in Chapter 8.

The pattern is easy to modify for fit: if you are smaller or larger around the waist and hips, simply subtract or add an equal amount at the side seam on both the back and front pattern pieces. Also adjust the length of the waist extension/casing at the side seam position, as indicated, by the same amount. If you have a generous derrière, you can increase the body depth by adding to the depth of the yoke and/or the corresponding seam on the back panel. For a tall person, add extra height to the body all around the yoke seam.

# Mompe ■ Materials and cutting notes

- Approx. 2.1m (2 ¼yds) of fabric, 114cm (45in) wide (more if you lengthen the pattern)

- Thread for sewing

- Elastic, 1cm (⅜in) wide, twice your waist measurement plus an extra 10cm (4in)

For pattern see page 108.

Cut out the pieces, using a layout to suit the fabric available. Fold the fabric in half so that the main pattern pieces can be cut on a double layer. For silk, place the top of the main pieces towards the same end of the yardage. After cutting the main pieces, fold a long remnant in half the other way to position and cut the waist extension/casing piece. Transfer markings before sewing.

## Assembling the mompe

- Seam allowances are 1.5cm (⅝in) except where otherwise stated.

- RS = right side, WS = wrong side, CB = centre back, CF = centre front

Optional pocket: cut one and press 1cm (⅜in) to WS on top edge for hem. Stitch, and then press under 1cm (⅜in) on remaining edges as marked on pattern. Position on front or back, right or left (depending on your preference) and sew before proceeding as below.

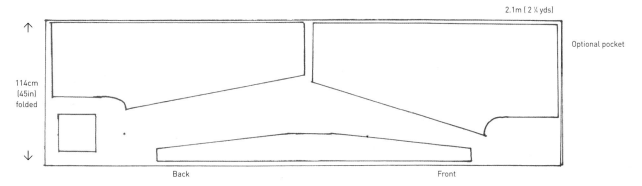

2.1m ( 2 ¼ yds)

Optional pocket

114cm
(45in)
folded

Back          Front

* Cut on double fabric, then refold to cut one waist extension

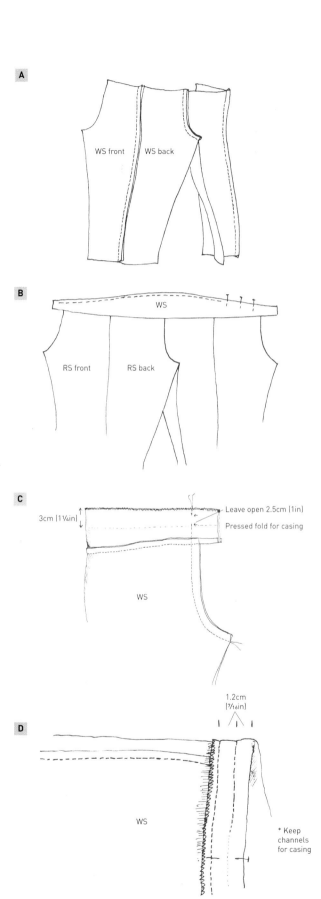

**A**

WS front    WS back

**B**

WS

RS front    RS back

**C**

3cm (1¼in)

Leave open 2.5cm (1in)

Pressed fold for casing

WS

1.2cm (7/16in)

**D**

WS

* Keep channels for casing

1. With RS together, join the CB seam, and then, with RS together, sew the fronts to the backs at the side seams only (fig A). Stop sewing 6cm (2⅜in) above the hem if vents are desired. Press seams and finish as wished.

2. With RS together, attach the curved edge of the waist extension/casing to the top of the leg unit (fig B). This pattern piece is drafted to be somewhat longer than may be needed, so expect to trim it once attached. Press seam towards waist then topstitch, 7mm (¼in) from seam on RS. Overlock or zigzag the remaining straight edge, unless it is a selvedge. Press 3cm (1¼in) to WS on straight edge ready to form casing.

3. Unfold pressed casing and sew CF seam, continuing onto casing but leaving a 2.5cm (1in) gap, as marked on pattern (fig C). Press CF seam open and topstitch on casing only, to make threading elastic easier. Refold casing in position.

4. Mark and work two parallel lines of stitching as evenly as possible, as shown on the casing pattern, to form two channels (fig D). Via CF seam opening, thread both channels with 1cm (⅜in) elastic, using safety pins attached to both ends. Try on the mompe and adjust fit of elasticated waist. Make a neat overlapping join in both bands of elastic and trim excess, allowing it to pop into casing.

5. Hem bottoms of legs by pressing 1cm (⅜in), then 2cm (¾in) to WS. Machine topstitch, including side seam allowances at vents if included.

6. With RS together, pin inside leg seams, matching at hemlines and body seam and easing back and fronts together as necessary. Sew and then press.

## Alternative finish

After pressing hems in place at step 5, go to step 6 and sew inside leg seams, unfolding hems to do so. Next, reposition hems and stitch in place. The first method makes machining the hems, especially with vents, easier for the less accomplished maker, but the second method is more traditional and unlikely to result in a 'step' at the inside seam.

# Drawstring version

At step 3 above, sew the entire centre front seam without a gap. At step 4, mark only the lower line of stitching indicated on the pattern. With the casing unfolded, on the area which will be within the casing on the outside of the body, work two buttonholes, about 3cm (1¼in) apart, one at each side of the CF seam. Refold the casing in position and stitch. From the main fabric, cut a drawstring, 6cm (2½in) wide and as long as your waist measurement plus about 75cm (30in). Fold in half lengthways, RS together, and sew the long seam, with 1cm (⅜in) turnings, stitching across at each end and leaving an opening of about 20cm (8in) for turning. Turn right side out, press and sew the opening closed. Then, with a safety pin, thread the drawstring through the buttonholes into the casing and centre.

## Tip

To turn drawstring RS out, cut strong thread to the same length as the drawstring fabric. Thread it through the eye of a safety pin and knot the ends together. Have this thread inside the folded fabric with the knot placed to be trapped when sewing this half of the drawstring. Pull gently on the safety pin and with something like a chopstick or knitting needle begin to push the end inside. It may be tricky getting started but once the end is inside, with a combination of steady pressure on the safety pin thread while running your hand the other way, you will soon make progress. About halfway, when the closed end appears at the opening, insert the chopstick and use this to ensure the corners at the end are turned out squarely (fig E). Continue to turn the rest of the tail out. Repeat for the other end. Press and sew the opening closed.

Incidentally, a Japanese chopstick is a better turning tool than a Chinese chopstick because it has a more pointed tip.

E

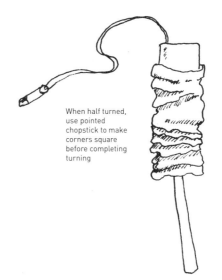

When half turned, use pointed chopstick to make corners square before completing turning

# CHAPTER 5 Hippari and jimbei

These two – the hippari and jimbei – are more or less female and male equivalents, similar in construction. The hippari is worn by women and resembles a short version of the kimono. It has a wrap-over front, though without the extensions of a kimono, and a collar that runs down to the hem. There may be an opening under the arms at the side seams, as with the kimono. Like the kimono, it always wraps left over right, but it fastens with two pairs of ties instead of a wrap-around sash. When overlapped and fastened, the fit is comfortably loose. Sleeves on a hippari can include both the straight or curved bottom edges from the conventional styles on kimono, but they never have the excessive length of kimono sleeves. They can be simply angled and may, as in the source garment shown here, have a narrow casing for elastic to provide a closer fit.

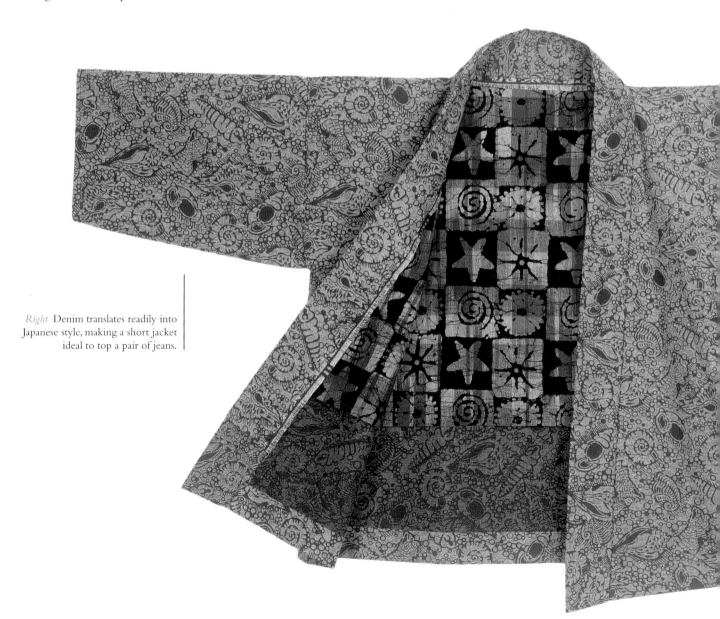

*Right* Denim translates readily into Japanese style, making a short jacket ideal to top a pair of jeans.

*Right* Hand-sewn, simply constructed, this garment features slightly shaped underarm seams and casings for elastic.

*Left* This sample hippari (matching the mompe) has shorter sleeves. A delicate wash of fabric paint was added to a couple of the printed roses.

The hippari can equate to a western blouse or a lightweight jacket, depending on the fabric chosen for making it. The examples illustrated here include a top with shortened sleeves to wear with the mompe from Chapter 4 as pyjamas or lounging wear. These are made in printed cotton lawn – cool and comfortable to wear as well as easy to launder. There is a shorter version without ties or underarm openings to wear as a jacket over jeans, made from a fabric similar in weight and colour to denim, but with a woven design of seashells, and partly lined with a batik print over a plaid ground. Several of the original garments that were studied before writing this book had part-linings. Perhaps simply an economy measure, these part-linings also provide an extra layer for warmth and support over the shoulders while adding no extra volume around the waist!

The main difference in the pattern for the jimbei, mainly worn by men, is that the collar finishes short of the hem, leaving a straight turned front edge. The jimbei never has an underarm opening. The source garment has a pocket on the inside of the left front, side vents with little facings and ties that are a bit longer than those of the hippari. Side vents are not merely style details, but serve the practical function of providing more room for movement around the hips when bending over or kneeling to work.

The source jimbei came as part of a pair, with a western-style waistcoat (vest) to wear over it, so this jimbei is designed to be worn as a shirt. However, with a T-shirt underneath, the very same garment can function perfectly well as a lightweight casual jacket.

*Left*  A commercial version of the traditional form provided the source pattern for our jimbei.

*Left* Contrast this unlined painted silk hippari with the pinstriped version, below, to appreciate the versatility of the garment.

# Hippari ■ Materials and cutting notes

- **Either** approximately 2m (2 ¼yds) of fabric, 114cm (45in) wide

- **or** 5.7m (6¼yds) of Japanese fabric, 35cm (14in) wide

For pattern see pages 110–111.

Cut out, with the patterns for body, sleeve, collar and ties, using a layout that best suits the fabric available. Vary the lengths of the sleeves or the body patterns, if necessary, to suit a length of fabric which you may already have.

## Seashell jacket version

- 1.36m (1½yds) of seashell denim, 114cm (45in) wide

- 90cm (1yd) of lining fabric, 114cm (45in) wide

On the seashell jacket, after a check to ensure that it would still fit the intended wearer, the width was also reduced by 3cm (1⅛in) in order to fit the pattern onto the cloth (fig A, page 66). If you are doing this, remember to take the same amount from both front and back. If adding a shoulder seam, add 1.5cm (⅝in) to both back and front, and likewise if there is a CB seam in the collar. Before removing the paper pattern, transfer markings to the fabric.

Approx 2.2m (2½ yards)
*Use a similar layout for jimbei

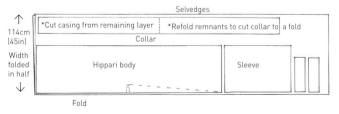

*Left* This pinstriped garment is fully lined like western jackets. Both these garments have a timeless quality, each dressy in its own way.

# Assembling the hippari

- Seam allowances are 1.5cm (⅝in) except where otherwise stated.
- RS = right side, WS = wrong side, CB = centre back, CF = centre front

*Note* These instructions include an underarm opening. To make hippari without an opening, see 'Lined variation without underarm opening', below.

**1**  With RS together, fold the ties in half lengthwise and sew with 6mm (¼in) seam allowances. Turn RS out and neaten one end of each by folding in a small turning and slip-stitching to close. Press.

**2**  On the body, cut across the back neckline as marked, stopping just short of the pivot point. Also cut down the CF line but do not trim away any fabric. Next, either stay-stitch neck pivot points at each side of the marked point (fig B), or sew the shoulder seams, if you have them, reverse-sewing at the pivot point ends to secure. (If you have shoulder seams, stay-stitching will not be necessary.)

**3**  On the collar, sew the CB seam if there is one and press open. Press 1cm (⅜in) to the WS along one long edge.

**4**  With RS together, taking a 1cm (⅜in) turning on the unpressed edge of the collar and following the stitching line marked on the pattern, match the CB collar to CB neck and pin outwards towards the left shoulder until the pivot point is reached. This is temporary, to ensure the collar is positioned as planned down the front. Now follow the instructions for attaching the collar to the kimono (page 52).

**5**  Press under doubled 1cm (⅜in) hems on the wrist edges of the sleeves and either topstitch by machine or hand sew invisibly. Alternatively, after pressing, wait until the underarm seam is stitched before sewing the hems.

**6**  With RS together and matching the midpoint of the sleeve to the shoulder-line of the body, sew the sleeves to the body, leaving 4cm (1½in) unstitched at each end (fig C).

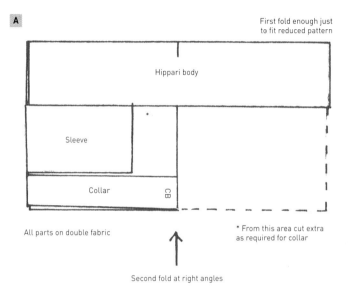

A

First fold enough just to fit reduced pattern

Hippari body

Sleeve

*

Collar

CB

All parts on double fabric

\* From this area cut extra as required for collar

Second fold at right angles

B

Cut up centre front and at neck almost to pivot points

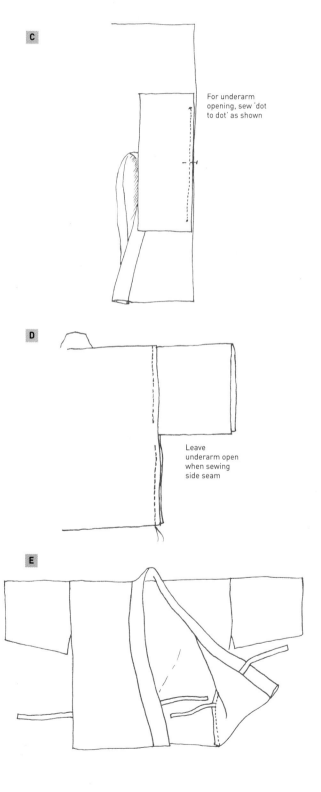

C

For underarm
opening, sew 'dot
to dot' as shown

D

Leave
underarm open
when sewing
side seam

E

**7** Fold hippari, RS together, across the shoulder-line to bring the raw edges of the sleeves and the body side seams together. Sew the side seams, leaving an underarm opening, as desired (fig D). Press.

**8** Along the hem edge, press 1cm (⅜in) to WS, then 2cm (¾in). Pin or tack (baste) in place. Fold in ends of collar, trimming to reduce bulk as required. Machine-hem from collar seam on one side to collar seam on the other side. Hand sew pre-folded edge of collar to stitching-line of collar on the inside and slip-stitch the ends.

**9** Sew the sleeve underarm seams towards the wrists: this can be as per the pattern, straight or tapered, or maybe with an alternative curve of your choice. Turn in the seam allowances narrowly at the underarm openings on both the sleeves and the body and stitch very lightly.

**10** Pin the ties to the points marked: approximately 40cm (16in) down from shoulder on inside left side seam and outside right, and approximately 47cm (18½in) from shoulder on inside collar front edges (fig E). Try on the hippari and check the fit. If necessary, adjust height of ties to suit before sewing neatly in place by hand or machine. The ties should not be fastened for such a close fit as to put undue strain upon them.

# Decorative option

Over the centuries, the Japanese have devised many ways to dye and paint cloth. Some are incredibly complex, yet the simplest approaches can still be worth exploring, particularly for the novice dressmaker. Fabric paints are readily available now and offer a way to individualize purchased fabrics. The simple printed lawn used for this hippari had a little delicate colour added to a couple of the motifs on the top left front.

Always read the manufacturer's instructions and follow them carefully, especially when fixing the painted fabric. Painting into an existing motif can be done quite freely; for best effect use a fairly chunky brush, such as a pastry brush!

# Lined variation without underarm opening

Lining may be partial, as on the seashell jacket, or full. To cut a partial lining, use the same pattern piece as for the body but shortened by an equal amount at both back and front. The length of lining may be limited by fabric availability but ideally should extend somewhat below the underarm point.

After cutting out, press 1cm (⅜in) to the WS on the lower edges of the lining back and front and stitch. Place lining WS to WS of the outer jacket, tack (baste) together, and then treat these layers as one during rest of assembly.

For a full lining, cut body and sleeves using the hippari pattern, then refer to the notes on making a lined kimono to make and attach this to the outer layer. Add the collar as the final step.

If making either garment without an underarm opening, as on the seashell jacket, at step 6, sew the sleeves to the body except for 1.5cm (⅝in) turnings at both ends. Press seams.

Fold the seam allowance of the sleeve clear in order to sew the side seam of the body from the end point of the sleeve seam towards the hem. Again keeping the seam allowance free from the seam, sew the seam on the sleeves. This avoids sewing across the intersection, allowing the turnings to fall as they will for pressing and comfort in wear.

*Left* A handsewn hippari, cropped short to the waist, inspired the seashell jacket (page 62). This garment also has a slightly curved underarm seam and a lining.

# Seashell jacket – decorative details

There are further details on this jacket, copied from vintage Japanese clothing.

**1** It may be necessary to make joins in the long strips of fabric required for collars on Japanese garments. In the west, collars are generally seamed at the centre back and there may be times when you find this is the best solution for the fabric you have left for cutting the collar. However, when the length is only a small amount short, you can copy the Japanese style of having three pieces, a central section and one at each side. Cut the overall length with sufficient extra for seaming the joins. If there is enough, copy another Japanese touch and, instead of pressing the joins open, press seams to one side with a small extra fold of fabric, resembling a tuck. This can appear more pleasing to the eye than a seam pretending it isn't there. The tuck adds a little texture and a sense of opulence rather than economy!

**2** One long edge of the collar has been cut as a selvedge (see page 62). This edge is not pressed under as at the beginning of step 3. Instead, when the jacket is complete it lies towards the body and is secured with a line of decorative stitching in bold cotton thread, hand-worked through both the collar layer and the garment, close to the collar seam. This selvedge allows the manufacturer's woven production lettering to be glimpsed as a decorative feature. In western dressmaking, it is usual to cut away the selvedge or to conceal it within a turning. However, the Japanese think that if something is required for the making process then it has a right to be there in the finished article. For this reason, if you put tacking (basting) into making something, in Japan you would not remove this at the conclusion as you would in the west. Tacking (basting) can often be found on vintage kimono panels. Probably the very same logic lies behind the visible selvedge.

**3** The same decorative stitching has been worked along the sleeve side of the seams, joining sleeves to body, again through both the outer fabric and its turning. On this garment, as on the one that inspired it, the stitching is worked in a dark thread. However, it is in the tradition of the textile art known as sashiko (see page 38).

*Left* Here you can see the bold navy stitching that holds the facing side of the collar in place.

# Jimbei ■ Materials and cutting notes

- 2.2m (2½yds) of fabric, 114cm (45in) wide

For pattern see page 112.

You may vary the lengths of the sleeves or the body patterns, if necessary, to suit a length of fabric which you may already have. Transfer markings before starting to sew.

## Assembling the jimbei

- Seam allowances are 1.5cm (⅝in), except where otherwise stated.

- RS = right side, WS = wrong side, CB = centre back, CF = centre front

**1** Attach the pocket first. Consider whether you wish to make it up with the WS of the cloth outwards so that it will blend with the inside of the front. Press under 1cm (⅜in) and then 2cm (¾in) on the top of the pocket and sew. Next, press under 1cm (⅜in) turnings on the remaining three sides of the pocket. Position on WS of left front panel and sew in place, reinforcing each top corner with a triangle of stitching (fig A).

**2** Begin as for the hippari, but after step 2 press in and stitch a narrow double hem on both straight front edges, below where the collar will be sewn. Continue the stitching above the clipped top of the turning until it crosses the diagonal where the collar will be.

**3** The collar on the jimbei illustrated here needed a CB seam in order to fit it into the available fabric. In this case, pin, sew and press this seam before attaching the collar. Begin by matching the CB seam to the CB neck to be sure the collar will be properly centred, but then sew as for the kimono (page 52), except that the collar finishes above the hem.

**A**

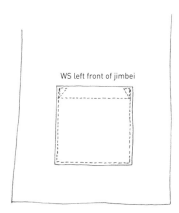

WS left front of jimbei

**B**

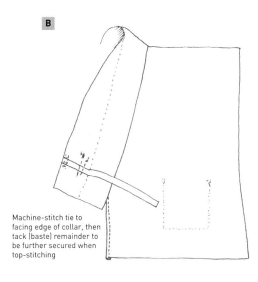

Machine-stitch tie to facing edge of collar, then tack (baste) remainder to be further secured when top-stitching

**4** Try on the jimbei, if possible, and check whether to adjust the height of the ties or follow the marked guidelines. Place one short tie on the RS of the right-hand seam of the back panel. Place the second short tie on the WS of the side seam of the left front. Sew the two long ties to the unfolded seam allowances of the collar, level with each other, and tack (baste) in position across what will be the inside face of the collar (fig B). Turn in the ends of the collar and topstitch all around, crossing the ties as you go. You may like to add a couple of lines of topstitching along the collar also.

**5** Return to the hippari instructions, step 6, to attach the sleeves, but following the notes for the version without an underarm opening. Leave 11cm (4⅜in) unstitched at the ends of the side seams, if you wish to have vents. With RS together, sew vent facing to the bottom ends of the side seam allowances and press.

**6** At the bottom hem, turn under 1cm (⅜in) and then 2cm (¾in), and press into place. Press the ends of the vent facings to be level with the hem. Turn in the outer top and side edges of the vent facings and press. Pin or tack (baste), then topstitch along hem and vents in one process.

# Decorative option

Conventionally, men's clothing is more understated than women's wear and is less likely to have decorative details. However, there are simple touches that can be added without feminizing the garment being made. The jimbei here has just such a variation. As both sides of the denim cloth were pleasing, it was decided to make up the collar with the 'wrong side' of the fabric outwards. When the garment is worn below the waistcoat, the effect of the contrast 'V' of the collar that is visible between the waistcoat collars is very stylish.

Of course, many fabrics are unsuited to being displayed this way, but occasionally you will be lucky enough to find fabric that is equally interesting on both sides.

Another small detail, also seen on the seashell jacket earlier, has been to use the selvedge, here when cutting the vent facings. This means those edges did not have to be turned in, making them less bulky and easier to sew.

*Right* Using both sides of the denim adds a simple touch of interest. The lighter side displays topstitching clearly.

# CHAPTER 6 Waistcoats

Waistcoats (vests) are worn by men, women and children in Japan. They offer an extra layer of warmth, without inhibiting movement. Sometimes, one can find a pair of garments in the same fabric, such as the man's jimbei (in Chapter 5) and western-style waistcoat, intended to be worn together, with the waistcoat on top.

Two adult versions of the garment are given: a traditional design, featuring side panels, which is suitable for use with narrow Japanese fabric and a style influenced by western patterns, which requires wider cloth. Both are roughly hip-length and have a straight collar right to the hem, with a pair of ties to keep the front under control. Both patterns have shoulder seams, making them especially suitable for use with fabrics which have either a nap or a design that has a right way up, such as the brocade with roses on the reversible woman's garment opposite. In this case, the collar may also be cut to keep the pattern in the correct direction by putting a seam at the centre back neck. Remember to add 1.5cm (⅝in) seam allowances where the pattern normally goes to a fold.

*Left* The waistcoat length, the cut around the armholes and how the collar sits all suit the intended wear over the jimbei, but it can slip happily over western shirts too.

*Right* A commercially made interpretation of basic garment forms features a western-influenced waistcoat. This appeared after Japan opened its borders in the 19th century.

*Above* Reversible waistcoats in neutral colours and timeless fabrics optimize wear. Pockets on the linen side are large enough to be useful.

Either version can be made to fit men or women. A traditional waistcoat could be a great way to use the brocade from an obi, if you are fortunate enough to have one. You would require a CB seam and so may need to add a 1.5cm (⅝in) seam allowance at the CB of the pattern.

Waistcoats are generally lined and may also be padded. Those of small children are usually heavily padded. Another useful alternative is an unpadded but reversible version. Japanese clothes traditionally do not have pockets, but because these are so useful, the patterns and instructions include pockets on the western-style waistcoat. If making a reversible version, add pockets on only one layer.

Take care to choose the correct instructions below for the style you require.

Three different patterns are given; the first two – a traditional lined waistcoat and a western-style waistcoat are sized for men and for women, but in practice you may make either design to either size. The third pattern, for the child's chan-chanko, is intended to fit a 3- to 4-year-old, if made as directed. The fit can easily be modified (see instructions).

*Left* This commercial version of a popular child's garment used black velvet for the trim and is cut including a small sleeve.

# Traditional lined waistcoat
## Materials and cutting notes

### Woman's size

- **Either** 2.6m (2⅞yds) of Japanese fabric, 35cm (14in) wide

- **or** 1m (1⅛yds) of outer fabric, 114cm (45in) wide

- 0.7m (¾yd) of lining fabric, 114cm (45in) wide

- Thread for sewing

For pattern see page 109.

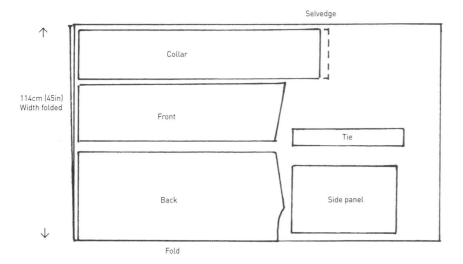

### Man's size

- **Either** 3.7m (4yds) of Japanese fabric, 35cm (14in) wide

- **or** 1.9m (2yds) of outer fabric, 114cm (45in) wide

- 1.4m (1⅝yds) of lining fabric, 114cm (45in) wide

- Thread for sewing

For pattern see page 114.

Cut out, using all patterns for body, collar and ties for the outer fabric, with a layout that best suits the fabric available. If using western fabric and omitting the CB seam, place the pattern to overlap the CB fold by 1.5cm (⅝in). Omit collar and ties for the lining. Transfer markings before starting to sew.

▪ Seam allowances are 1.5cm (⅝in) except where otherwise stated.

▪ RS = right side, WS = wrong side, CB = centre back

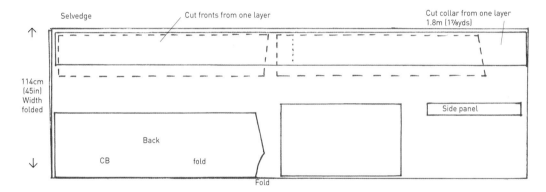

*Right* A traditional waistcoat with a 'boxy' form, low under the arms, that could have been worn over kimono.

## Assembling the traditional lined waistcoat

1  Join CB seam if you have one. Place fronts to back with RS together and sew shoulder seams. Press seams open. Repeat for lining.

2  Place these two, RS together, on a flat surface, matching shoulder seams at neck and armhole edges. Pin layers together between the side panel points on back and front and across hems. Sew pinned seams (fig A). Do not sew the front neck edge. Turn RS out and check that the sides will be level at the hems when completed; if so, press.

3  Align shoulder seams on the neck edge then pin and tack (baste) the outer and the lining together within the seam allowance of 1cm (⅜in). This tacking can stay in.

4  With RS together, sew collar CB seam. Press open. Press 1cm (⅜in) turning to WS along one long edge.

5  Matching CB collar seam to CB on neck edge, with RS together and taking a 1cm (⅜in) seam allowance, pin the collar to the garment all the way, and then sew. Press seam allowances towards collar and trim one layer to reduce bulk if wished.

6  Make ties as directed for the hippari (see page 66). Pin and sew to the seam allowance of the collar, approximately 15cm (6in) up from the hem (or at your preferred point), so that when the pressed edge of the collar is sewn in place, the ties will project. Pin the pressed edge of the collar in position and hand sew, turning in the ends level with the hem as you go.

7  Place one side panel, RS together, with one side panel lining; pin top edge (underarm) and hem edge, and then sew (fig B). Turn RS out; check fit with side panel position on garment, then press. Repeat for second panel. Tack (baste) the long sides of both panels within the seam allowances so they will behave as one.

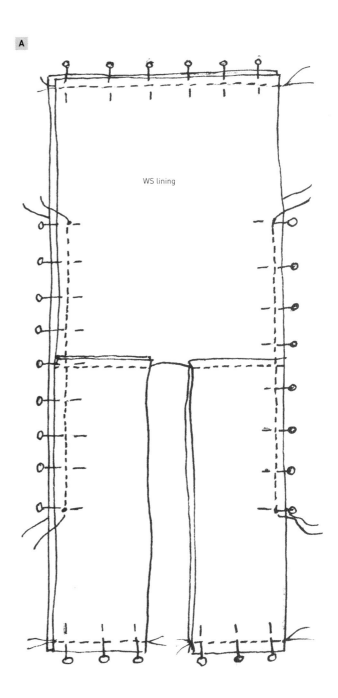

A

WS lining

When sewing dot to dot be accurate to ensure side panels will fit. Secure ends of stitching by knotting threads, reverse-stitching or sewing a few stitches on 'O' setting

**8** With RS together, aligning the top of one side panel with the side panel point on the front and keeping the front lining clear, pin the lined side panel to the outer fabric front (fig C). Stitch through all three layers, still keeping front lining clear, and press turnings towards front. Repeat to attach the second side panel to the other front. Then repeat the process to join the sides to the back. Press turnings towards back. Turn in the front and back linings over the seams and hand sew to finish.

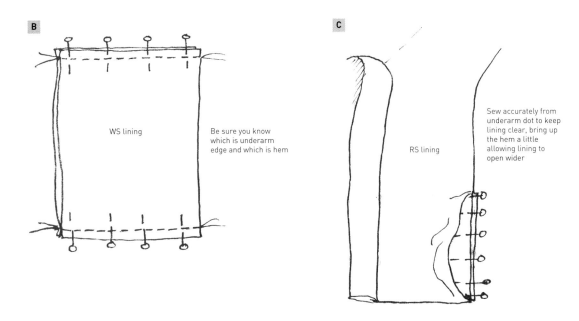

B

WS lining

Be sure you know which is underarm edge and which is hem

C

RS lining

Sew accurately from underarm dot to keep lining clear, bring up the hem a little allowing lining to open wider

## Decorative options

Perhaps it is stating the obvious, but fabrics such as this glittery example provide plenty of visual interest without demanding embellishment. Although we suggest ways to decorate and personalize garments, this does not imply that it is necessary in all cases. This waistcoat fabric is made with a warp of alternate black and gold lurex threads while the weft is a fairly unevenly-spun and space-dyed silk. The disproportion between these threads makes a fabric that is chunky and rather unstable. It works well in the simple panels as required for this garment, but would not make very successful ties. A gold-coloured slubbed silk remnant was therefore chosen for the collar guard (Chapter 9) and the ties.

*Left* Silk rouleaux are twisted together with a few strands from the weft of the garment fabric to make unusual ties.

# Lined western-style waistcoat
## Materials and cutting notes

### Woman's size

- **Either** 3m (3⅜yds) of Japanese fabric, 35cm (14in) wide

- **or** 1.3m (1½yds) of outer fabric, 114cm (45in) wide

- **either** the same amount of the reverse fabric

- **or** 70cm (¾yd) of lining fabric, 114cm (45in) wide

- Thread for sewing

For pattern see page 117.

### Man's size

- 1.9m (2yds) of outer fabric, 114cm (45in) wide

- **either** the same amount of the reverse fabric

- **or** 1.7m (1⅞yds) of lining fabric, 114cm (45in) wide

- Thread for sewing

For pattern see page 118.

Cut out, using the patterns for body, collar and ties, with a layout that best suits the fabric available. This pattern was designed to be placed on a CB fold with no extra seam allowance. Body patterns alone are required for lining. Transfer markings before starting to sew.

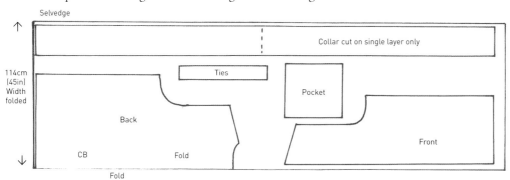

A

WS lining

Sew accurately for
top edge of vents

Avoid stretching
curve as armhole
is sewn

B

RS lining

RS outer fabric

Seam allowances pressed towards lining

# Assembling the lined western-style waistcoat

- Seam allowances are 1.5cm (⅝in) except where otherwise stated.

- RS = right side, WS = wrong side, CB = centre back

1  Hem top of pockets by pressing turnings, as marked, to the WS and stitching. Press under turnings on one side and lower edge, making a pair. Position on the appropriate front panel with the unpressed edge level with the side seam and stitch the pressed edges carefully. Tack (baste) pockets to side seams.

2  Make ties as directed for hippari (see page 66).

3  With RS together, sew fronts to matching back at shoulders. Press seams open. Repeat for the lining.

4  Place these two units with RS together on a flat surface and pin around the armholes and at side vents, as shown, if you wish to have them. Sew with 1.5cm (⅝in) turning at armholes and side vents (fig A). Clip the curves around the armholes. Turn RS out and press carefully. To prevent the lining around the armhole from rolling towards the outside of the garment, you may understitch the edge. Do this after pressing by separating the main layers and folding the seam allowance towards the lining. Stitch through these layers (not including the outer fabric) about 3mm (⅛in) from the seam, (fig B).

5  Tack (baste) layers together around back neck and front openings.

6  Prepare and attach collar as for traditional waistcoat, above.

7  Position one tie at each side of the front on the collar stitching line, about 21cm (8¼in) up from the hem, with the raw edge placed so that it will be enclosed in the finished collar. Machine in place, stitching through collar seam allowances only. No stitching should be visible on the RS of the collar.

**8** With outer fabric RS sides together and, keeping the lining layers free, pin from the underarm seam down to the top of the side vent or to the hem edge and sew (fig C). Repeat on the second side. Press the seam and then, folding one lining layer neatly inside and turning the other in 1.5cm (⅝in) over it, hand sew invisibly in place.

**9** Treating lining and outer as one layer, press up hem as marked and machine-stitch. Turn up and press the ends of the collar to be level with the garment hem. Trim if required and sew neatly by hand. Blind-stitch the long pressed edge of the collar in place to the machine stitching that attaches the collar.

## Assembling the reversible western-style waistcoat

As above, but with the following extra notes:

**1** Reversible version cutting note: cut a pair of ties in one fabric only and a pair of pockets in one fabric only. In our example (shown page 73), the ties are in brocade, the pockets in linen. The collar may either be entirely of one fabric or, as with our example, you might choose to cut half the collar width in brocade and half in linen. In this case, add a 1cm (⅜in) seam allowance down the entire length of the collar.

**2** In our example, linen pockets were sewn to linen fronts, but you could switch fabrics, having brocade pockets on linen fronts, for example, depending on the look you want or the fabric available.

**3** When placing the two layers RS together, for pinning around the armholes, also pin and sew across the back and front hems. If you wish to have side vents, mark as shown for stitching. Sew these seams with 1.5cm (⅝in) turnings at armholes and side vents, but only 1cm (⅜in) at hems. Clip the curves around the armholes and trim the corners at side vents diagonally. Turn RS out and press carefully. Do not understitch either fabric.

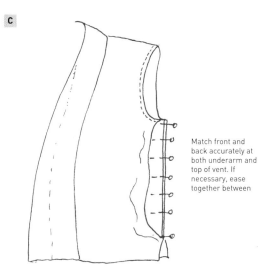

C

Match front and back accurately at both underarm and top of vent. If necessary, ease together between

**4** Collar preparation may vary according to fabric choice. If you are using one fabric, cut as pattern piece, simply press under 1cm (⅜in) on one long edge. If collar is to feature both fabrics and have a CB seam, first make the CB seam on both fabrics and press open. Next, place brocade and linen collars RS together and sew down one long edge. Turn RS out and press seamed edge crisply. Press 1cm (⅜in) to WS on one fabric only – for example, linen. Matching brocade collar to brocade side of garment, attach collar as directed for traditional waistcoat.

**5** With brocade sides together and keeping the linen layers free, pin from the underarm seam down to the top of the side vent and sew. Repeat on the second side. Press brocade seam and then, tucking front linen layer neatly inside, turn the back in 1.5cm (⅝in) over it. Hand sew invisibly to complete the reversibility of the garment.

# Decorative options

Vintage Japanese textiles often have embroidered details added to woven or dyed designs. They are frequently worked in stitches that are simple enough even for the beginner, such as the couching and satin stitch seen on the beautiful sample of a sleeve illustrated here.

Inspired by them, one motif of the brocade on each of the waistcoat fronts is accented by simple embroidery (see page 82). Running stitch in ivory-coloured silk thread was worked first and has then been whipped using a metallic machine embroidery thread.

Adding emphasis to the existing pattern of a purchased fabric is a great way to give it a unique touch. It does not require the artistic skills that you might need to create your own designs, since you only need to follow what is already there. If the fabric is lightweight, fuse a patch of lightweight iron-on interfacing or tack (baste) a piece of Stitch'n'Tear to the WS of the area to be embroidered. This keeps the fabric flat and helps you to work stitches with an even tension. An embroidery hoop also helps with this aspect, if you have one.

Western embroiderers often tend to cover the whole panel, if not the whole garment, with stitchery, but Japanese design generally favours a minimalist approach where 'less is more.' A few well-placed accents would be more in character with Japanese fabrics, though of course in the end, as maker, you must always please yourself.

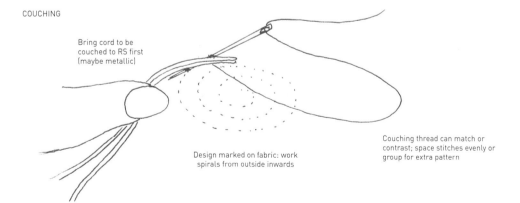

COUCHING

Bring cord to be couched to RS first (maybe metallic)

Design marked on fabric: work spirals from outside inwards

Couching thread can match or contrast; space stitches evenly or group for extra pattern

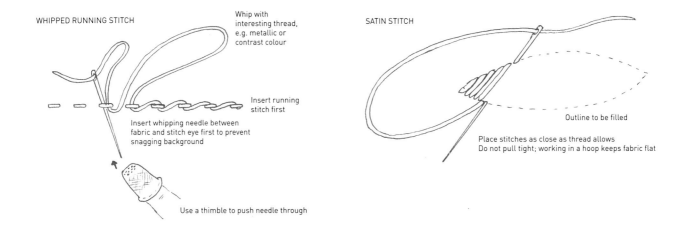

WHIPPED RUNNING STITCH

Whip with
interesting thread,
e.g. metallic or
contrast colour

Insert running
stitch first

Insert whipping needle between
fabric and stitch eye first to prevent
snagging background

Use a thimble to push needle through

SATIN STITCH

Outline to be filled

Place stitches as close as thread allows
Do not pull tight; working in a hoop keeps fabric flat

*Left* Before stitching, hold the
garment panel up to you to
decide whether the motif can
be seen and is flattering to you.

# Child's chan-chanko
## Materials and cutting notes

- 1.15m (1¼yds) of outer fabric, 114cm (45in) wide; you will only require a minimum of 80cm (⅞yd) if direction is not a problem

- 20cm (¼yd) of contrast fabric, 114cm (45in) wide

- 70cm (¾yd) of lining fabric, 114cm (45in) wide

- 70cm (¾yd) of wadding (batting)

- Thread for sewing

For pattern see page 116.

Cut out, using the patterns for body, collar, pockets and ties for the outer fabric, with a layout that best suits the fabric available. From contrast fabric, cut collar cover, pocket trim and sleeve binding. From lining, cut back, fronts and pocket linings. Cut the wadding later, following the instructions on page 102. This pattern was designed to be placed on a CB fold with no extra seam allowance.

Transfer the markings for the shoulder tucks to the RS of the garment fronts and back. Tiny dots with a silver dressmaker's pencil, showing just the beginning and end of the lines, will be sufficient.

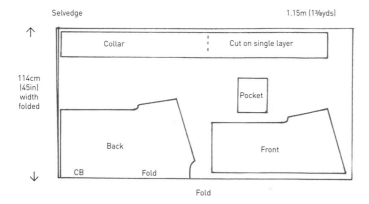

*Above* Besides being a felicitous colour, red would
help you spot your child in a crowd!

# Assembling the child's chan-chanko

- Seam allowances are 1.5cm (⅝in) except where otherwise stated.

- RS = right side, WS = wrong side, CB = centre back

**1** Fold pocket contrast trim in half, RS out, and position along the top of the pocket, raw edges level. Place a pocket lining, RS together, on top and sew with a 1cm (⅜in) turning. Press lining to WS of pocket. Topstitch pocket trim close to folded edge. Press 1cm (⅜in) turning to WS on one side and lower edge. Repeat to make a second pocket, but for the other hand. Position pockets on fronts, as indicated, having raw edge level with side edge of front, and stitch. Tack (baste) layers at side seams.

**2** Make ties as for hippari (see page 66).

**3** On the contrast collar cover, press under 1cm (⅜in) twice at each short end and topstitch. If the main collar is cut with a CB seam, join and press open. With RS of the main collar up, centre the contrast collar, also RS up, over the CB seam and tack (baste) in place down the long edges, within the turning. Press under a 1cm (⅜in) turning on one long side. Unfold this to position the ties, with raw edge level with collar edge at the points marked. Topstitch the tie almost halfway across the collar; turn and sew across the tie width, and then turn and sew back to the raw edge (fig A). Put aside until needed.

**4** Place front linings to back lining and sew at sides and shoulders. Press seams open.

**5** Place garment fronts to back and sew at shoulders. Press the whole unit, as wrinkles remaining now will be difficult to remove later without damaging the wadding. Add the wadding to the body panels, following directions on page 102. Also cut wadding to fit the sleeve bindings and the collar.

**6** Place the contrast sleeve binding along the sleeve edge, RS together, and sew with a 1cm (⅜in) seam allowance.

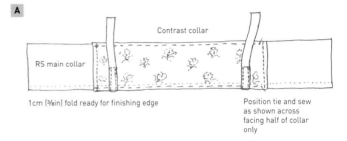

**A**

RS main collar

Contrast collar

1cm (⅜in) fold ready for finishing edge

Position tie and sew as shown across facing half of collar only

If the wadding catches on the presser foot or feed-dog, try inserting a narrow strip of tissue paper to cover the wadding. Tear away after sewing. Press lightly (so as not to flatten wadding) away from the body, but do not finish off the binding yet. Repeat with second sleeve.

**7** With RS together, bring the fronts and back together at the side seams and, including the sleeve bindings, sew the seams through all layers. Lightly press the side seams open at the hem.

**8** Place lining to body with RS together along the hem edge and sew with a 1cm (⅜in) turning (fig B, page 86). Turn RS out and press the turning towards the lining, again avoiding crushing the wadding. Now fold the lining inside the garment, bringing the shoulder seams to match at neck and armhole edges. This will automatically fold the hem up to the correct position.

Do not press the hem into a sharp edge – a bouncy rolled edge is a characteristic of this garment. Pin and tack (baste) the lining to the wadded outer fabric all around the neck and front opening.

**9** Attach the collar as for the traditional waistcoat. Avoid catching the ties in the seam. Roll the collar to the inside of the garment, keeping a rounded edge, and hand sew to the machine stitching on the inside, turning up the ends level with the hem.

**10** Turn the garment inside out. Roll the sleeve bindings to the inside; pin and tack (baste). Turn in 1cm (⅜in) on the sleeve edges of the lining; overlap this over the binding, and slipstitch in place. Remove tacking thread.

**11** To make this garment fit the small shoulders of the child, the final step is to sew the shoulder tucks. Fold the garment along the centre tuck line marked, bringing together the outer and inner lines on the front and continuing over the shoulder seam to the back markings. Load a needle with double thread and make a bold knot. Begin at one end of the line with your knot, taking bold stitches on one side and short ones on the other; stitch between the marks, drawing the layers together securely (fig C). Repeat on the other shoulder. As the child grows, these tucks can be made narrower. They may also be unpicked for laundering and resewn when dry. The girth of this garment will fit older children but the pattern can easily be made wider by redrawing the side seam further out.

## Re-sizing note

To make the garment for a taller child, calculate how much extra length is required then divide this amount in two. One half of the measurement should be added by drawing a line across the garment at the midpoint of the sleeve and opening up the pattern here by the required amount. The remaining half can be added to the hem.

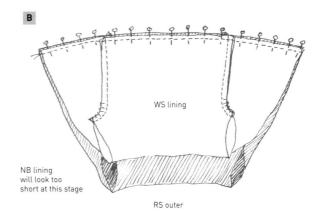

B

WS lining

NB lining will look too short at this stage

RS outer

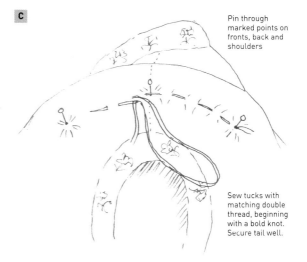

C

Pin through marked points on fronts, back and shoulders

Sew tucks with matching double thread, beginning with a bold knot. Secure tail well.

*Right*  Hand-stitched boldly to complete the garment, the shoulder
tucks are adjustable for growth.

# CHAPTER 7 Hanten

Hanten are worn as a jacket or coat by both men and women. The source garments show that different lengths and sleeve styles are possible. The underarm seams are completely closed and the front does not wrap over in the way that the kimono does. However, if you make the version where the collar attaches to the front with a sloping seam, then the effect is for the collar to overlap itself (as with kimono, arrange the left side over the right). The other style has a straight line from the neck point to the hem for attaching the collar, so it always hangs open. Neither garment has ties or other fastenings.

Both source garments were hand-sewn. The longer one is made throughout of two layers of fabric densely stitched together in the technique called sashiko, the stitches being worked in dark thread and simply following alternate fine stripes in the weave of the cloth. This strengthens the fabric considerably. As there is no lining, one can see that the stitching follows the convention of having the long threads all starting and ending in a regular position across the panel.

The other hanten features printed characters down the collar and on the back. This example is shorter, having a very deep hem without side vents. The sleeves have contrast facings.

*Left* Compare the differences between this hanten and the one on the opposite page: the slight variation in attaching the collar, the alternative underarm angles and the different lengths.

*Right*  Inside the hanten, we see
how the sashiko stitching shows a
horizontal line of knots, due to
working with lengths of thread
from a skein cut at a single point.

The gift of a couple of Indonesian sarongs inspired our interpretation. Neither was sufficiently long to make the complete garment and the two fabrics did not exactly match each other. The most creative option, if combining them, was to incorporate areas of patchwork, using an existing collection of pieces to create a versatile 'coat of many colours'. The method uses a foundation fabric for each pattern piece and the patchwork is assembled to cover the required area (see page 34). It is simple enough for any of the garments in the book and very practical, as all the seams of the piecing are covered, leaving a neat inside to the garment.

*Left* Fabrics such as sarongs may be printed in ways that need thoughtful planning to make best use of them. Be content to exploit the Japanese preference for asymmetry sometimes!

*Right* Instead of patchwork, a hanten of plain fabric could have a single large motif on the back.

The pattern drafted here suits fabric of Japanese width. If you use western fabric and omit the CB seam, you must therefore place the pattern pieces to overlap the centre fold by 1.5cm (⅝in), where necessary. You are also likely to cut back and front separately to make handling the panels for piecing simpler, so must add 1.5cm (⅝in) seam allowances on the shoulder-line of both back and fronts. For an unpieced garment, use the quantity of fabric required for the foundation.

# Hanten ■ Materials and cutting notes

- **Either** 6.2m (6¾yds) of Japanese fabric, 35cm (14in) wide; shorter version 5.8m (6⅜yds)

- **or** 2.6m (2¾yds) of foundation fabric, 114cm (45in) wide

- Two sarongs or yardage

- Scraps for patchwork

- Thread for sewing

For pattern see page 120.

Cut out the foundation, using the patterns for body and sleeves, with a layout that best suits the fabric available. From the sarong fabric, plan how to make best use of the printed design to fit into your garment panels. Cut two collars: one from foundation fabric plus one from one of the sarongs. Transfer markings before starting to sew.

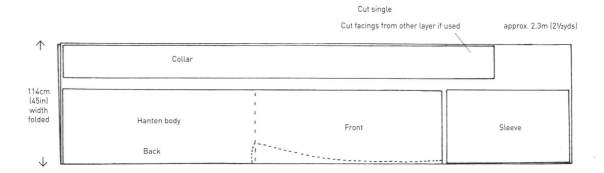

## Assembling the hanten

- Seam allowances are 1.5cm (⅝in) except where otherwise stated.

- RS = right side, WS = wrong side, CB = centre back, CF = centre front

**1** Having cut the pattern pieces, assemble the patchwork to your chosen design. The example here features just one strip of piecing between two wider full-length strips of sarong fabric. Your design may be different, according to the fabric available. However, as a general rule, vertical designs are more flattering than horizontal elements. After pressing, tack (baste) all the long edges together so the layers will behave as one during construction of the garment.

**2** With RS together, match back and fronts at shoulders and sew. Press seam open.

**3** If the collar has a seam at CB, sew this now and press open. To make the weight of the collar consistent with the rest of the garment, tack (baste) the foundation fabric collar to the WS of the collar fabric. Press a 1cm (⅜in) turning to the WS along one long edge.

**4** With RS together, position the CB of the collar to the CB neck of the garment and, taking a 1cm (⅜in) seam allowance, pin all the way around the collar to ensure it will be correctly centred. Attach as for the kimono (see page 52). Hand sew the inside edge of the collar to the stitching, leaving a short amount free until the hem is made.

**5** Decide on the position of the underarm seam, if you have not already done so, and mark. If you wish to have facings on the sleeves, position these, RS together, on the wrist edges and sew, taking a 1cm (⅜in) turning (fig A). Press and understitch (as directed in the western-style waistcoat, page 79), if wished. Alternatively, press and sew narrow hems on the sleeves.

**A**

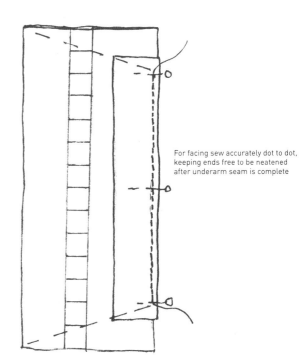

For facing sew accurately dot to dot, keeping ends free to be neatened after underarm seam is complete

Chosen and marked underarm seam

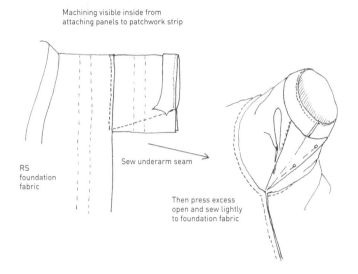

B

Machining visible inside from
attaching panels to patchwork strip

RS
foundation
fabric

Sew underarm seam

Then press excess
open and sew lightly
to foundation fabric

**6** Matching the halfway point of the sleeve to the shoulder seam on the garment, and with RS together, pin and sew the sleeves to the body. Press the seams, and then sew the underarm seam (fig B). Press the seam open and, if you have tapered the sleeve, later catch-stitch the extra fabric invisibly to the foundation along with the facing.

**7** Match the side seams of the body, with RS together. Sew and then press.

**8** Try on the garment, checking where the hem should come. Turn in ends of the collar level with the hem and trim if necessary. Press into place and sew either invisibly by hand or by machine.

## Decorative option

Besides the pieced exterior of this garment, there is another low-key decorative element inside. Instead of using ordinary lining fabric or muslin, a hand-dyed shibori fabric has been chosen.

Shibori is an ancient textile art of shaped resist dyeing (see pages 40–46). Many of its methods involve stitching, although pleating, folding, clamping and wrapping are also employed. The fabric used here was decorated with a few circles filled with different patterns of stitching and dyed in two separate colours to add a subtle dimension to the final result.

*Right* To the left of the hanten lining is a length of vintage shibori, sold with gathers unpressed so that the buyer knows it is not a printed imitation.

# CHAPTER 8 Haori

The haori (say it like 'dowry') may be worn by men or women. About three-quarter-length, it is often colour-coordinated to the kimono ensemble, like a dress-and-coat outfit, rather than a garment to wear anytime. It has ties, but remains open at the front, revealing the kimono below. The collar is worn turned over at the back and folded away from the collar seam.

The source garment is made from powder-blue silk jacquard, adorned with a few sprigs of cream and gold decoration. It is beautifully hand-sewn throughout. Even if a haori is machined, its construction demands more hand finishing than other garments. This example has a part-lining of cream silk shaded with pink clouds and the rest of the lining is achieved by extremely deep hems. This necessitates long body panels, so you may decide to 'westernize' by cutting both outer and lining with 5cm (2in) hems and hemming each separately. Alternatively, you might cut outer and lining to your desired length and construct as for a lined kimono.

Haori may be unlined and, for summer, could be of gauze – the type that provided the inspiration for the sample garment. Made from printed georgette bought at a sari shop, this would be stylish over a swimsuit. For a more dressy effect, it could be worn with drawstring mompe (page 58), plus a camisole. Unlined sheer garments need to be well finished inside, so are more suitable for experienced makers.

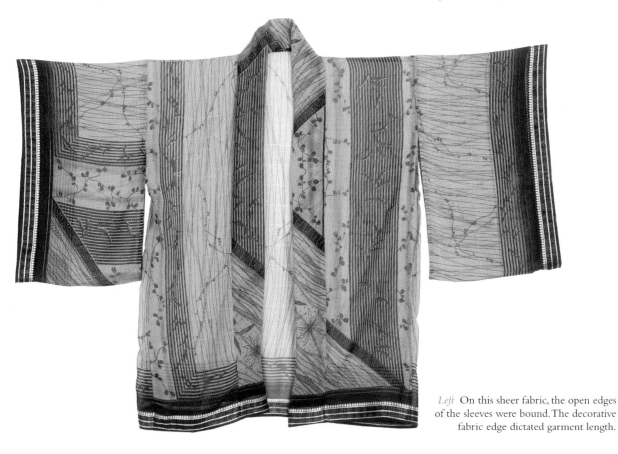

*Left*  On this sheer fabric, the open edges of the sleeves were bound. The decorative fabric edge dictated garment length.

*Left* This elegant haori has an exceptionally deep hem, ensuring that in wear only the main fabric would be seen.

*Left* The back view shows how the collar is folded in half at the back, unlike any other Japanese garment.

# Haori ■ Materials and cutting notes

- **Either** 10m (11yds) of Japanese fabric, 35cm (14in) wide

- 4.2m (4⅝yd) of lining, 35cm (14in) wide

- **or** 3.6m (4yds) of fabric, 114cm (45in) wide

- 2m (2¼yds) of lining fabric, 114cm (45in) wide

- Thread for sewing

For pattern see pages 122–123.

The pattern drafted here suits Japanese-width fabric. If you use western fabric and omit the CB seam, you must place the pattern to overlap the centre fold by 1.5cm (⅝in). If you cut back and front separately for easier handling, add 1.5cm (⅝in) seam allowances to the shoulder-line at the back and fronts. Cut lining, using modified body, sleeve and side panel patterns. Transfer markings before starting to sew.

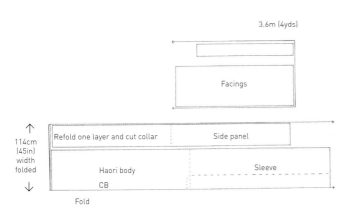

# Assembling the haori

- Seam allowances are 1.5cm (⅝in) except where otherwise stated.

- RS = right side, WS = wrong side, CB = centre back, CF = centre front

**1** Making the haori is similar to making a lined kimono, without extensions but adding side panels. Making the collar is the last step. Decorate the panels before assembling the garment.

**2** Work to kimono step 4 (see pages 52–56) but omit extensions on both outer fabric and lining.

**3** Attach outer fabric sleeves as step 6. Prepare sleeve linings as for a lined kimono.

**4** Place side panel outer and lining RS together and sew at the underarm. Turn RS out and press, as shown. Also press under the lining hem, as marked (fig A).

**5** Keeping the lining free, place one side panel RS together with the side seam of the front, matching the underarm point and noting that the side panel is tapered. Sew the seam as far as the hem fold, and press away from side panel. Repeat on the second front, then join to the back seams, also pressing away from side panel. Do not trim excess fabric from panels.

**6** Press up the outer fabric hems on the side panels (fig B, left). Pin then lightly catch in place. Overlap the side panel lining over the hem (fig B, right) and blind-stitch in place. Press up remaining outer fabric hems along their folds.

**7** Insert the body lining, WS together, pinning at neck and sleeves. Settle back and front hems in place and catch-stitch across the top. Hand sew the sides of the front and back hems turned in over the existing seams and fold the lining over them. This lining should be level at front and back but is above the side panel linings. Sew the lining to the top of the hems.

**8** Add sleeve linings as directed for kimono. If facings are desired, slip the lining inside the sleeve, WS together, and tack (baste) together around the wrist opening. Place facing RS together at the opening and sew as for the hanten, step 5 (page 92). Press the facing to the inside. Catch-stitch edges to lining.

**9** Tack (baste) the layers together around the neck edge within the seam allowance and add the collar as for the lined kimono, except that the inside edge overlaps the seam by an extra 7mm (a generous ¼in) to help the collar fold back over the fronts in the desired position. Therefore press under 1.75cm (scant ¾in) instead of 1cm (⅜in) when directed to prepare one edge and before finding the halfway fold for the collar. When finishing the collar, sew under this fold.

**10** The ties on the source haori are cords, which are attached to loops of fine rouleau. If you choose this method, add the loops before finishing the collar edge, about 43cm (17in) above the hemline. On the centre back collar, work a horizontal line of herringbone stitch where it rolls over, without coming to the RS (fig C).

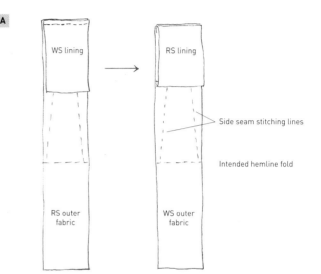

A

WS lining

RS lining

Side seam stitching lines

Intended hemline fold

RS outer fabric

WS outer fabric

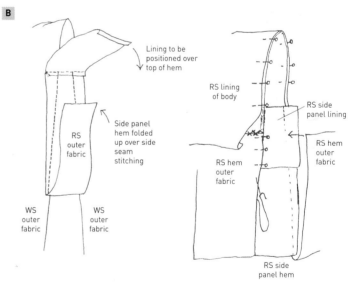

B

Lining to be positioned over top of hem

Side panel hem folded up over side seam stitching

RS outer fabric

WS outer fabric

WS outer fabric

RS lining of body

RS side panel lining

RS hem outer fabric

RS hem outer fabric

RS side panel hem

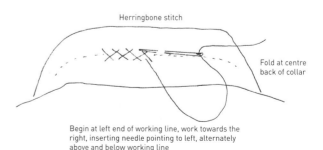

C

Herringbone stitch

Fold at centre back of collar

Begin at left end of working line, work towards the right, inserting needle pointing to left, alternately above and below working line

# CHAPTER 9 Additional pieces

## Collar guard

The introduction relates how kimono were taken apart for washing and explains that consequently this did not happen frequently. Nevertheless, clothing becomes marked, particularly around the neck, so the Japanese invented the collar guard. This extra piece of fabric is tacked (basted) over the fixed collar of the garment but is easily removed for washing. To make it inconspicuous, the guard is often made from the main fabric of the kimono or the same fabric as the main collar, if that is a contrast to the body. Alternatively, for everyday wear, the collar guard could have been black.

A collar guard could be a single layer of fabric, simply turned in and sewn on, but this would be challenging to wash, because it would be likely to fray. The following instructions are therefore for a bagged-out collar guard.

To make a collar guard, choose a fabric and use the original collar pattern piece, but shortened to about two-thirds of its length for garments such as waistcoats, hanten or haori. If possible, avoid a CB seam. Cut the guard about 2.5cm (1in) wider than the pattern. Using this as a pattern now, cut a second layer, either from the same fabric or from lining.

*Left* This gold silk collar guard is hand-sewn over the main garment collar.

**1** Place the two fabrics, RS together and, taking a 1cm (⅜in) allowance, sew around the rectangle, leaving an opening for turning RS out (fig A). Clip a triangle of fabric from each corner then turn RS out and press. Take care to achieve good square corners and to roll the seam right to the edge for a crisp appearance.

**2** Slip-stitch the opening closed.

**3** Fold the collar guard in half to find the centre and match this to the CB of the collar, positioning it so that one long edge of the collar guard will align with the outer seam of the collar to the body. Pin in place and fold the collar guard over the collar towards the inside of the garment. It should overlap the inside seam somewhat (fig B).

**4** Hand sew the outer edge of the collar guard into the groove as invisibly as possible. Then sew inside, following the edge of the collar rather than the edge of the collar guard.

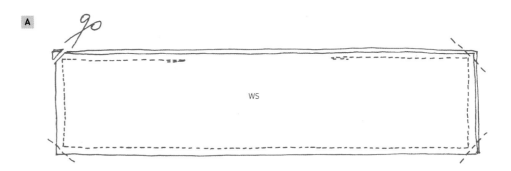

A

WS

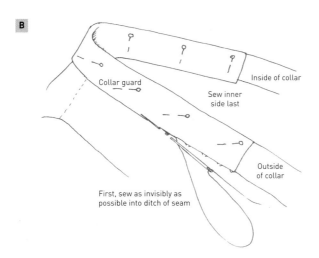

B

Collar guard

Inside of collar

Sew inner
side last

Outside
of collar

First, sew as invisibly as
possible into ditch of seam

# Mock obi

Instead of the elaborate obi or its opposite extreme, the simple sash, you may choose to make this design for a mock obi. It should be worn only by women and with the curved edge of the front panel to the top. The centre panel is bagged out, but the ties can be made from a single layer with a narrow hem, or a double layer, also bagged out. Use either a single fabric for all parts or choose a contrast lining.

Cut out, using the patterns provided on page 124: you need an outer and a lining for the front panel, plus two ties, either of single fabric or with a lining. The front panel is best if interfaced or wadded.

1  Decorate the front panel in any way you wish: for example, you might add an inserted strip of patchwork, apply a motif such that as used on the kimono, or work a quilted pattern.

2  For single ties, turn in and stitch a narrow hem all around, except on the end marked for pleating. For double ties, place a lining and an outer tie RS together and sew, with a 1cm (⅜in) seam allowance. Turn RS out and press. Form the box pleat across the end of each tie and tack (baste) in place.

3  Position one tie across a short end of the decorated front panel, RS together, ensuring that the sides are clear of the seam allowance on the panel, and tack (baste). Sew across the end twice within the seam allowance. Repeat with the second tie on the other end of the panel. Fold the ties up like a concertina and pin as shown, to avoid sewing in accidentally (fig A).

4  Place the panel lining over the decorated centre panel, RS together, and pin. Leaving an opening centrally on the straight lower edge, sew all around the remaining sides, as shown, taking a 1cm (⅜in) seam allowance (fig B). Turn RS out, unpin the ties and hem the opening closed.

**A**

After making up ties, form pleat and match to notch. Sew across twice within seam.

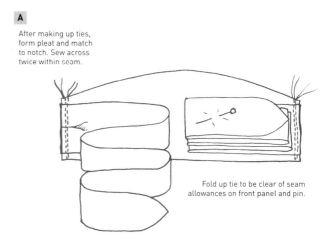

Fold up tie to be clear of seam allowances on front panel and pin.

**B**

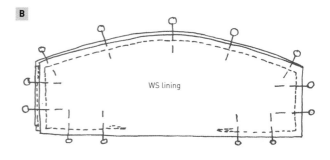

WS lining

# Ties

Ties are important details on many Japanese garments as they are the most widely-used method of fastening found on traditional clothing. Ties on period garments may be beautifully worked cords, but unless you already have learned the art of making these, you are most likely to be making fabric ties for the garments in this book.

In Japan, flat ties are somewhat casual and on a formal garment a round tie is more desirable. Most garments featured here can have flat ties, but for something like a haori or the brocade waistcoat, a round tie provides the type of quality detail the Japanese would prefer.

1   Cut ties of the length and width given for the pattern. Fold RS together and sew the long seam as usual, reversing stitching at both ends so it will not unravel. Turn RS out.

2   Cut just over twice the tie length of quilting wool or other suitable filling and thread through the tie, leaving a small extra tuft at one end and having the threader clear at the other. Cut the threader free, leaving some excess filling.

3   Load a needle with matching embroidery silk and make a firm knot in the end. Insert the needle near the seam inside the tube, as far from the end as you wish the binding to be: for example, 1cm (⅜in).

4   Pull the needle through to the outside and run tiny gathering stitches all around the fabric of the tube at this level (fig A). Returning to the seam, gather up as tightly as possible to form a 'waist' then take a small stitch or two to anchor.

5   Now wrap the silk around the tube exactly over the 'waist' 3 or 4 times – make a note how many you decided to do, if you want to make a matching pair! Again, take an anchoring stitch by the seam to prevent the wrapping coming loose.

6   Next, work buttonhole stitch over the wrapping all the way around (fig B; also shown on pages 104–105). Having completed the circuit, secure thread with a couple of tiny stitches pulled tightly under the binding to conceal them and cut thread.

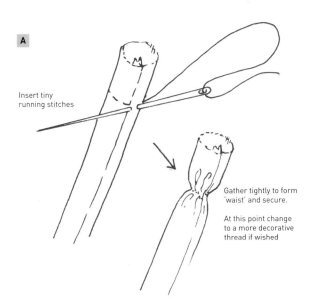

A

Insert tiny running stitches

Gather tightly to form 'waist' and secure.

At this point change to a more decorative thread if wished

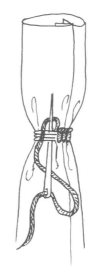

B

Wind thread around 'waist' then cover winding with densely worked buttonhole stitch

**7** Trim the excess filling and, if wished, fray the end of the fabric.

It is tempting to put more filling into the tube but beware of over-filling as this can make the ties too resilient to lie well when you tie the garment on. Soft, flexible ties are more sympathetic to wear.

As handmade cords were formed from threads rather than fabric, they were consequently not exactly the same as the garment. They could be a matching colour or a tasteful contrast, so they offer a precedent for the modern maker to experiment with an accent of colour or a textural contrast.

# Working with wadding

The most likely project for making with a layer of wadding (batting) is the child's chan-chanko, so the following instructions use this as an example. The basic procedure can be applied to other garments.

The traditional filling would have been silk. A number of cocoons would have been teased out to form as even a layer as possible over the garment to be covered. It was not quilted to secure it in position in the way that western quilted garments needed to be, because silk fibres cling to fabric with a kind of stickiness that cotton or wool fibres do not possess. The silk was usually added after the main parts of the garment were assembled, though before the lining was added. This meant that there were no extra layers contained at seam allowances and also that seams did not have a bouncy quilted appearance, as they would if wadded and then stitched.

In devising the following working method, I have attempted to retain some of the Japanese qualities, while recognizing that polyester wadding is the most likely product to be used.

**1** Have garment back and fronts sewn together at the shoulders and pressed.

**2** From the same paper pattern used to cut the fabric, cut a piece of wadding for each part, back and both fronts. For the chan-chanko, to give the authentic rolled hem, cut the wadding a little shorter than the full pattern, about halfway across the hem allowance. Use a double layer if you cannot buy the thicker wadding generally characteristic of these garments.

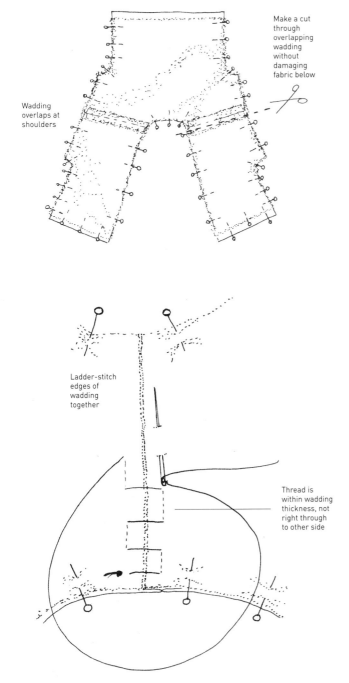

WS outer fabric (back)

Make a cut through overlapping wadding without damaging fabric below

Wadding overlaps at shoulders

Ladder-stitch edges of wadding together

Thread is within wadding thickness, not right through to other side

**3** Spread the assembled fabric layer flat on a work surface, RS down. Place the wadding panels over their respective fabric counterparts and pin at intervals around the edges. This produces an overlap at the shoulder seams. The seams will now be butted instead of seamed.

**4** Where the layers overlap at one shoulder, make a cut through both wadding layers positioned away from the fabric seam, a little nearer the front or the back, whichever seems best. If you have a double layer of wadding, butt the two layers together separately, having them fall one each side of the fabric seam. Remove the trimmings. Load a moderately large needle with a long piece of thread and work ladder stitching, as shown, stitching alternately from one side to the other across the butted join. You need a really chunky knot at the beginning of the thread to stop it pulling through the fibres. The needle should be going into the thickness of the wadding rather than right through to the other side. Do not pull the thread so tightly as to make dents in the wadding nor a ridge where the cut edges come together. The join should have exactly the appearance of the surrounding surface – no gaps, no lumps or bulges.

**5** After joining the wadding over both shoulders, tack (baste) the layers together around the edges of the garment panels, within the seam allowances. This saves having to remove the tacking later. Across the hem area, make a line of tacking that will be taken out later, just below the expected hem line. Next, along the cut edge of the wadding, pull and tease it into a softer edge. This prevents a hard edge being visible through the fabric when the hem is turned up later.

**6** Return to the assembly procedure and treat the wadded garment as if it were one layer. This method means you will need to sew the side seams through the wadding as well, but they are less conspicuous than the shoulder seams, which will have the authentic Japanese look. After sewing them, trim some of the wadding away to a thinner layer along the seam allowances.

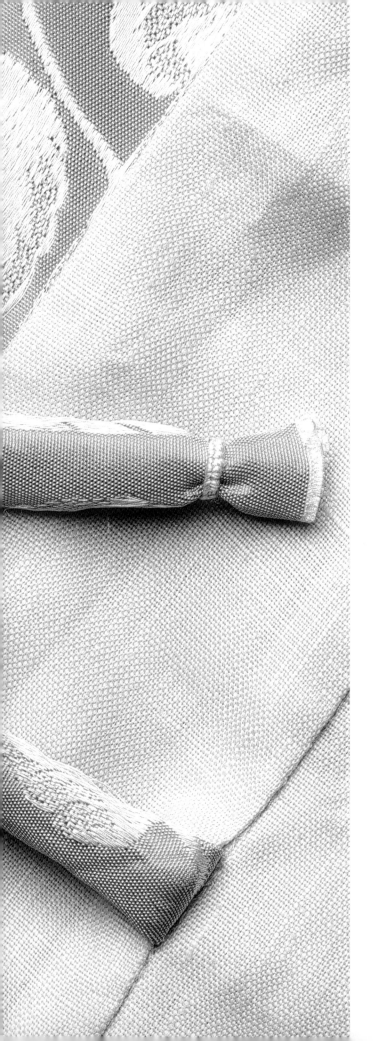

# THE PATTERNS

This section contains patterns for the garments which you will need to draw out at full size. With the exception of the kimono, all patterns have been shown at the same scale. The kimono is an exception because there is no need for a paper pattern. Instead we have provided two suggested layouts for fitting the rectangular pieces into a length of fabric. In order to fit these onto the page, they are represented at a different scale. You may use these layouts as a guide for devising your own to suit the fabric available.

For your convenience, all the most important measurements are printed on the patterns. This saves you much tedious counting of squares and hopefully reduces the possibility of errors. Taking time to read the numbers correctly and then to draw the lines carefully should ensure satisfactory results. Remember to mark all cutting notes and placement marks for efficient use at the construction stage. It is useful to see pattern drafting as not only the practical means to an end but equally valuably as a way to familiarize oneself with the form of the garment being made. Further notes on cutting out are to be found on pages 14-15.

# Kimono pattern design

This plan shows the measurements for the panels. Adjust lengths to suit individual projects.

SCALE: 1cm square on diagram = 10cm on garment.

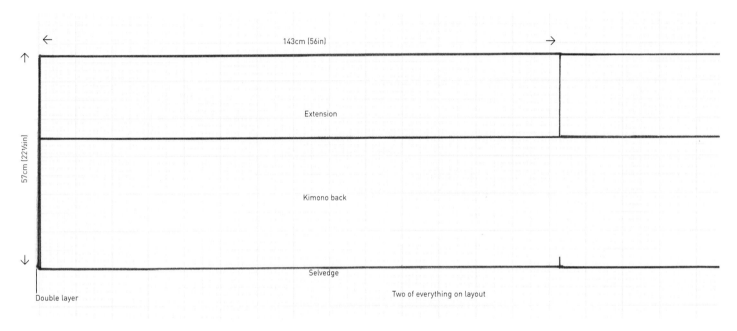

143cm (56in)

57cm (22½in)

Extension

Kimono back

Selvedge

Double layer

Two of everything on layout

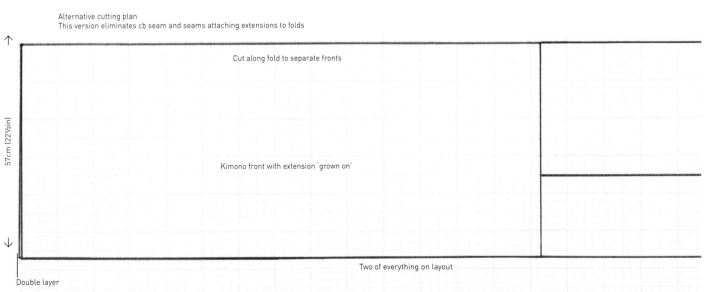

Alternative cutting plan
This version eliminates cb seam and seams attaching extensions to folds

57cm (22½in)

Cut along fold to separate fronts

Kimono front with extension 'grown on'

Double layer

Two of everything on layout

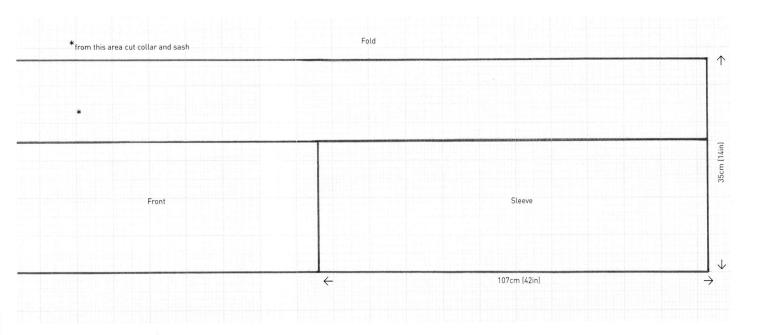

*from this area cut collar and sash

Fold

*

Front

Sleeve

35cm (14in)

107cm (42in)

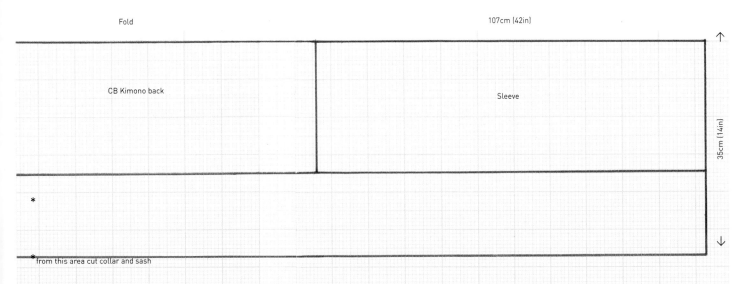

Fold

107cm (42in)

CB Kimono back

Sleeve

35cm (14in)

*

*from this area cut collar and sash

# Mompe

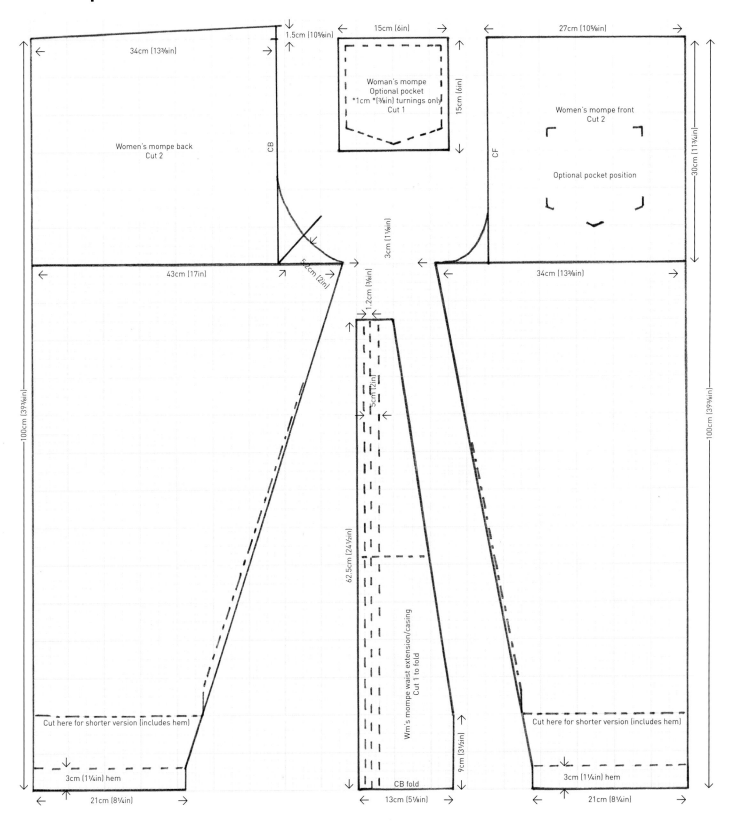

# Woman's traditional waistcoat

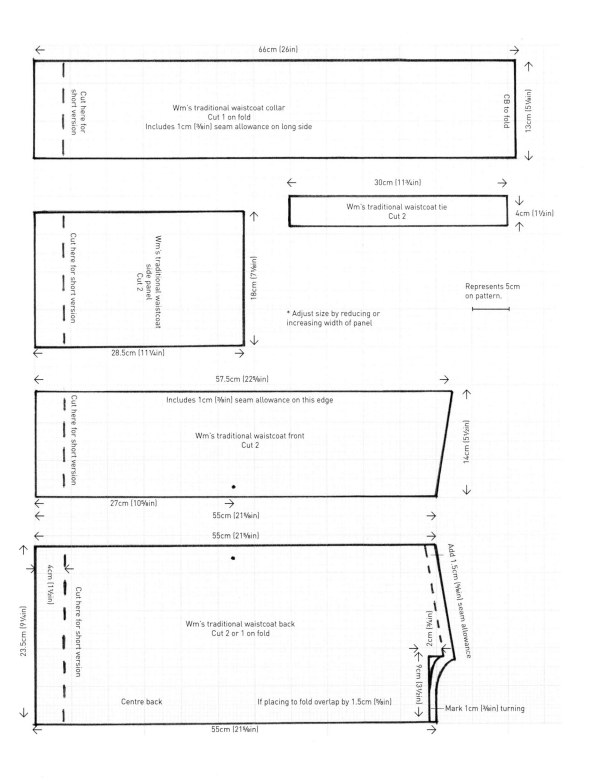

66cm (26in)

Cut here for short version

Wm's traditional waistcoat collar
Cut 1 on fold
Includes 1cm (⅜in) seam allowance on long side

CB to fold

13cm (5⅛in)

30cm (11¾in)

Wm's traditional waistcoat tie
Cut 2

4cm (1½in)

Cut here for short version

Wm's traditional waistcoat
side panel
Cut 2

18cm (7⅛in)

Represents 5cm
on pattern.

* Adjust size by reducing or
increasing width of panel

28.5cm (11¼in)

57.5cm (22⅝in)

Includes 1cm (⅜in) seam allowance on this edge

Cut here for short version

Wm's traditional waistcoat front
Cut 2

14cm (5½in)

27cm (10⅝in)

55cm (21⅝in)

55cm (21⅝in)

4cm (1½in)

Cut here for short version

Add 1.5cm (⅝in) seam allowance

Wm's traditional waistcoat back
Cut 2 or 1 on fold

23.5cm (9¼in)

2cm (¾in)

9cm (3½in)

Centre back

If placing to fold overlap by 1.5cm (⅝in)

Mark 1cm (⅜in) turning

55cm (21⅝in)

# Hippari

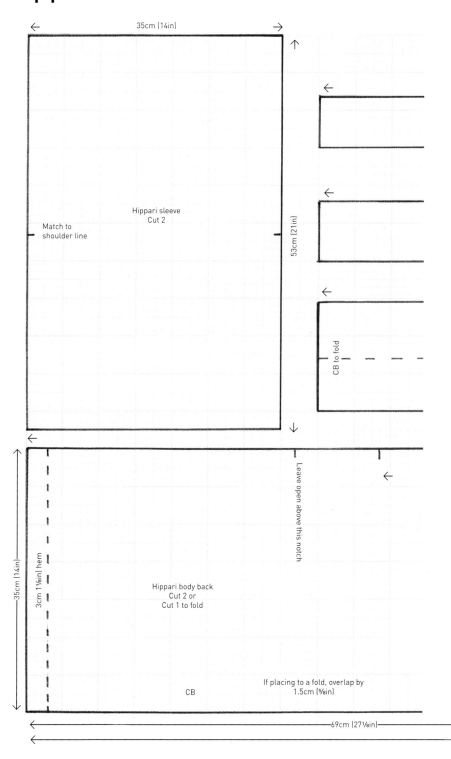

35cm (14in)

53cm (21in)

Hippari sleeve
Cut 2

Match to
shoulder line

CB to fold

Leave open above this notch

35cm (14in)

3cm (1⅛in) hem

Hippari body back
Cut 2 or
Cut 1 to fold

CB

If placing to a fold, overlap by
1.5cm (⅝in)

69cm (27⅛in)

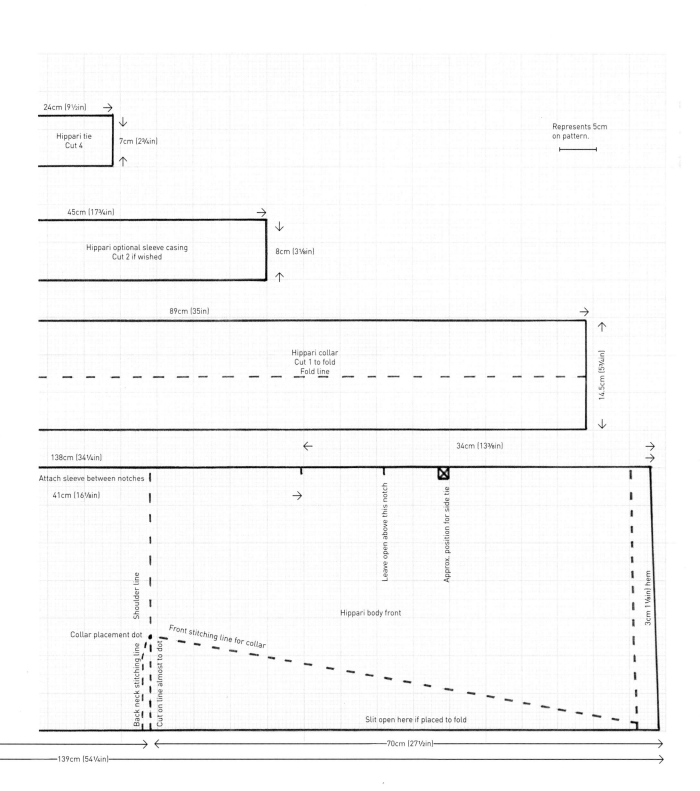

# Jimbei

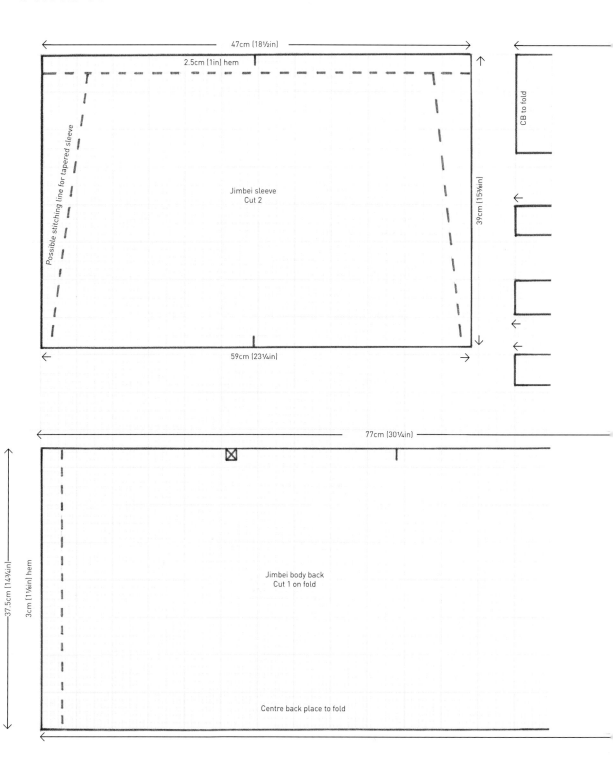

47cm (18½in)

2.5cm (1in) hem

Possible stitching line for tapered sleeve

Jimbei sleeve
Cut 2

39cm (15⅜in)

59cm (23¼in)

CB to fold

77cm (30¼in)

37.5cm (14¾in)

3cm (1⅛in) hem

Jimbei body back
Cut 1 on fold

Centre back place to fold

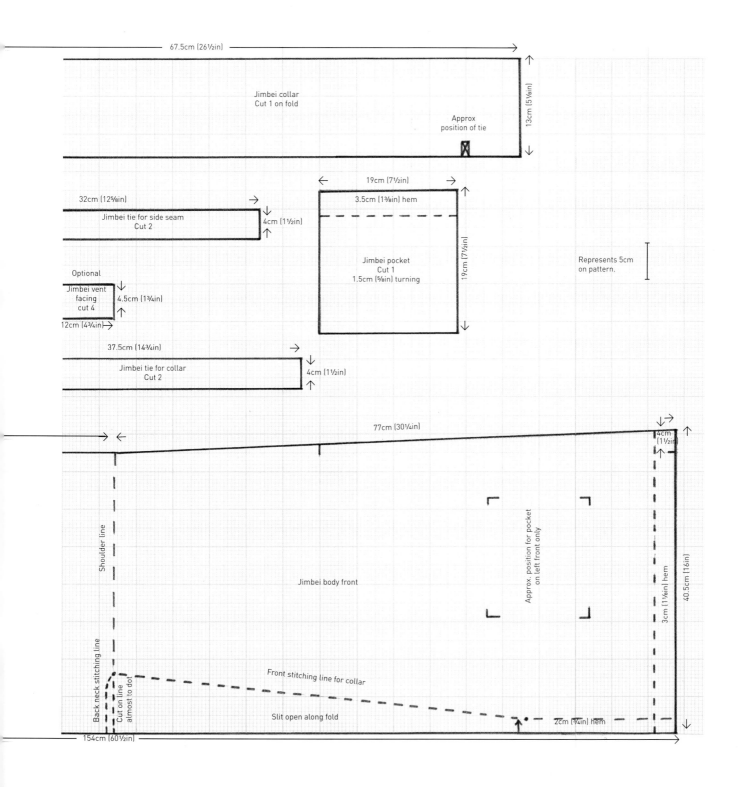

67.5cm (26½in)

Jimbei collar
Cut 1 on fold

Approx
position of tie

13cm (5⅛in)

19cm (7½in)

3.5cm (1⅜in) hem

32cm (12⅝in)

Jimbei tie for side seam
Cut 2

4cm (1½in)

Jimbei pocket
Cut 1
1.5cm (⅝in) turning

19cm (7½in)

Represents 5cm
on pattern.

Optional

Jimbei vent
facing
cut 4

4.5cm (1¾in)

12cm (4¾in)

37.5cm (14¾in)

Jimbei tie for collar
Cut 2

4cm (1½in)

77cm (30¼in)

4cm
(1½in)

Shoulder line

Jimbei body front

Approx. position for pocket
on left front only

3cm (1⅛in) hem

40.5cm (16in)

Back neck stitching line

Cut on line
almost to dot

Front stitching line for collar

Slit open along fold

2cm (¾in) hem

154cm (60½in)

# Man's traditional waistcoat

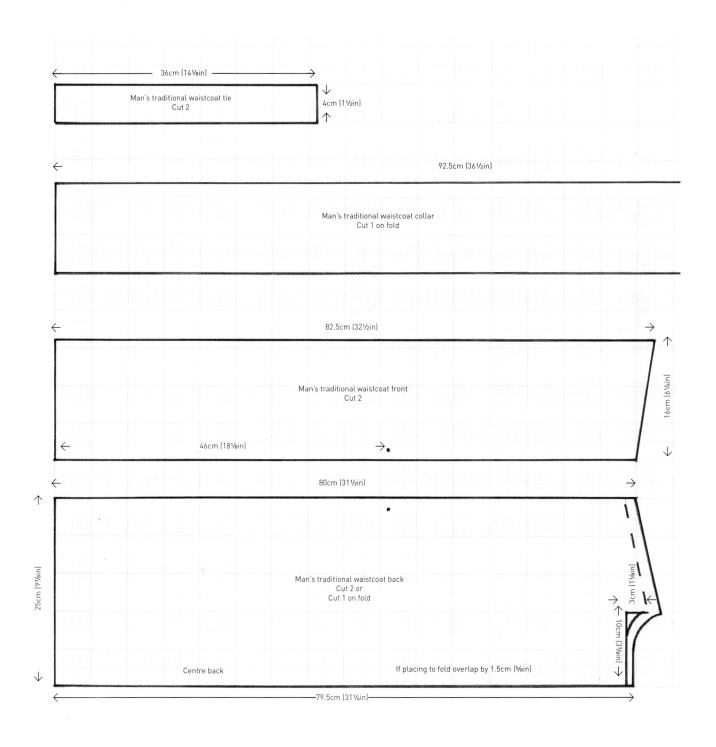

36cm (14⅛in)

Man's traditional waistcoat tie
Cut 2

4cm (1½in)

92.5cm (36½in)

Man's traditional waistcoat collar
Cut 1 on fold

82.5cm (32½in)

Man's traditional waistcoat front
Cut 2

16cm (6¼in)

46cm (18⅛in)

80cm (31½in)

25cm (9⅞in)

Man's traditional waistcoat back
Cut 2 or
Cut 1 on fold

3cm (1⅛in)

10cm (3⅞in)

Centre back

If placing to fold overlap by 1.5cm (⅝in)

79.5cm (31¼in)

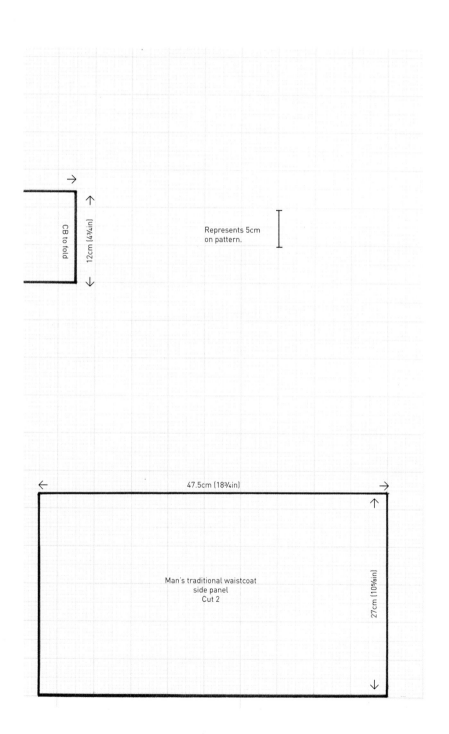

CB to fold

12cm (4¾in)

Represents 5cm
on pattern.

47.5cm (18¾in)

Man's traditional waistcoat
side panel
Cut 2

27cm (10⅝in)

# Child's chan-chanko

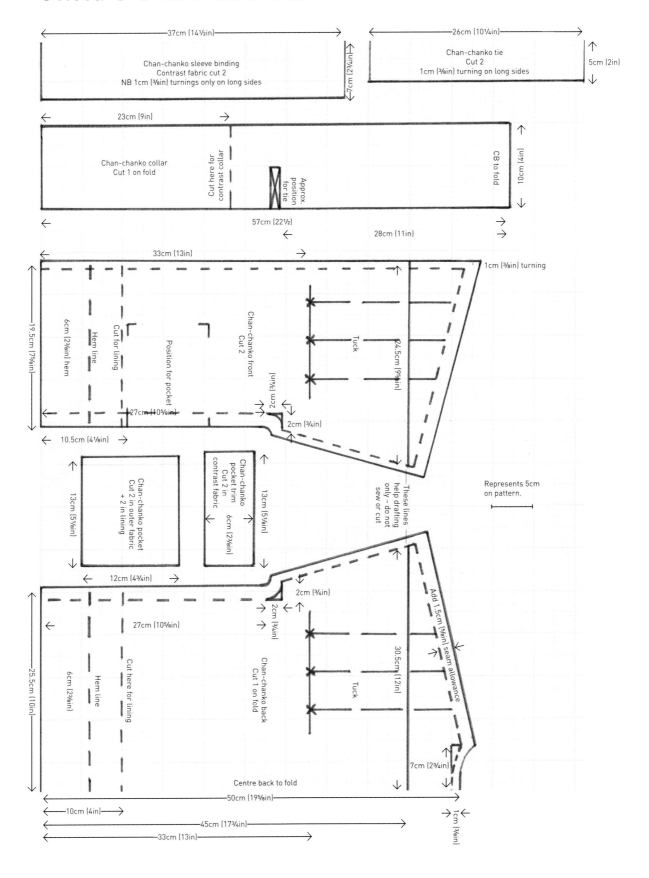

37cm (14½in)

Chan-chanko sleeve binding
Contrast fabric cut 2
NB 1cm (⅜in) turnings only on long sides

7cm (2¾in)

26cm (10¼in)

Chan-chanko tie
Cut 2
1cm (⅜in) turning on long sides

5cm (2in)

23cm (9in)

Chan-chanko collar
Cut 1 on fold

Cut here for contrast collar

Approx. position for tie

CB to fold

10cm (4in)

57cm (22½)

28cm (11in)

33cm (13in)

1cm (⅜in) turning

19.5cm (7⅝in)

6cm (2⅜in) hem

Hem line

Cut for lining

Position for pocket

Chan-chanko front
Cut 2

Tuck

24.5cm (9⅝in)

27cm (10⅝in)

2cm (¾in)

2cm (¾in)

10.5cm (4⅛in)

These lines help drafting only – do not sew or cut

Represents 5cm on pattern.

13cm (5⅛in)

Chan-chanko pocket
Cut 2 in outer fabric
+ 2 in lining

12cm (4¾in)

13cm (5⅛in)

Chan-chanko pocket trim
Cut 2 in contrast fabric

6cm (2⅜in)

2cm (¾in)

2cm (¾in)

Add 1.5cm (⅝in) seam allowance

30.5cm (12in)

27cm (10⅝in)

25.5cm (10in)

6cm (2⅜in)

Hem line

Cut here for lining

Chan-chanko back
Cut 1 on fold

Tuck

Centre back to fold

7cm (2¾in)

1cm (⅜in)

50cm (19⅝in)

10cm (4in)

45cm (17¾in)

33cm (13in)

# Woman's western-style waistcoat

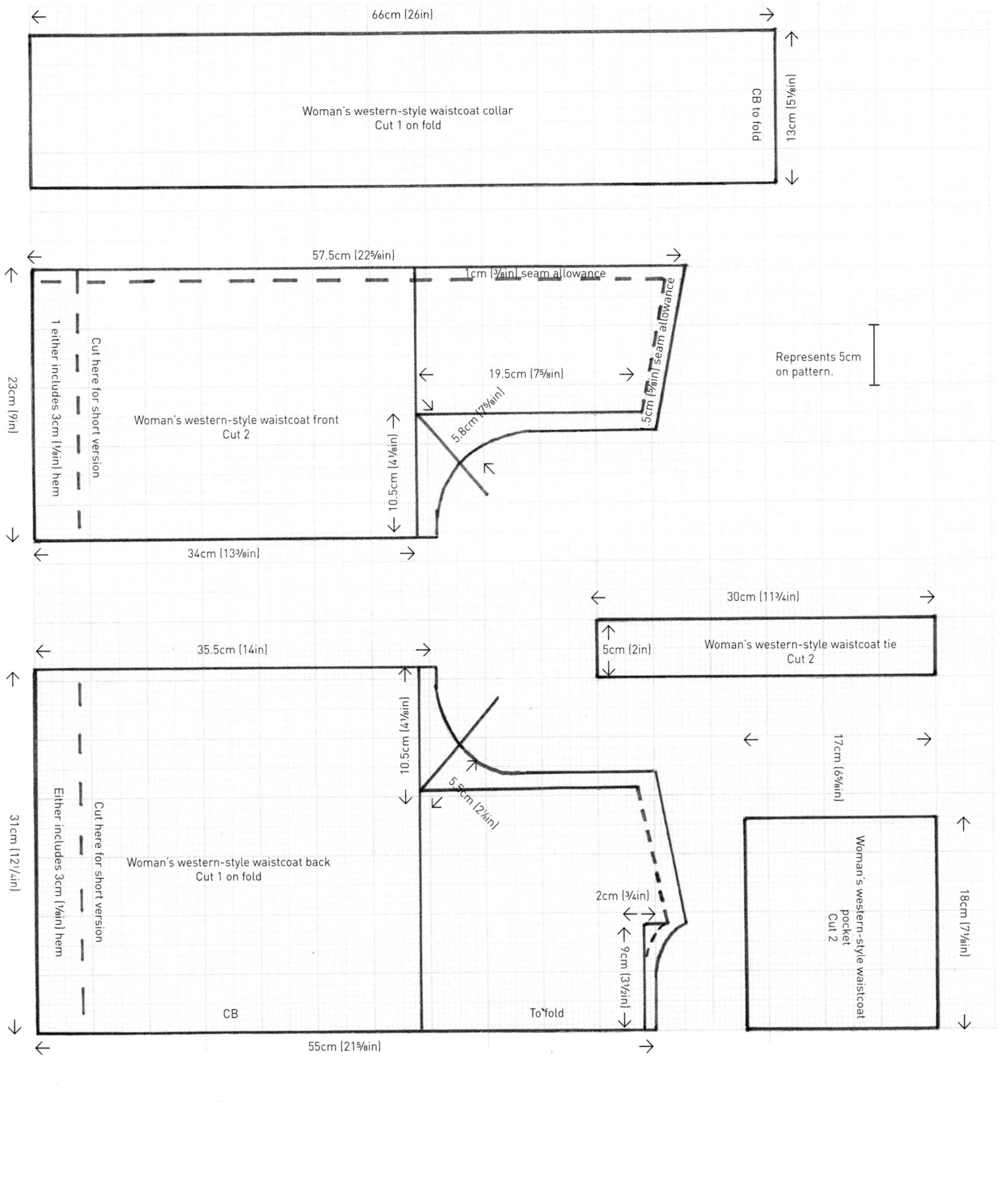
66cm (26in)
13cm (5⅛in)
CB to fold
Woman's western-style waistcoat collar
Cut 1 on fold
57.5cm (22⅝in)
1cm (⅜in) seam allowance
1.5cm (⅝in) seam allowance
23cm (9in)
Cut here for short version
1 either includes 3cm (1⅛in) hem
Woman's western-style waistcoat front
Cut 2
19.5cm (7⅝in)
5.8cm (2⅝in)
10.5cm (4⅛in)
34cm (13⅜in)
Represents 5cm on pattern.
30cm (11¾in)
5cm (2in)
Woman's western-style waistcoat tie
Cut 2
35.5cm (14in)
10.5cm (4⅛in)
5.5cm (2⅛in)
31cm (12¼in)
Cut here for short version
Either includes 3cm (1⅛in) hem
Woman's western-style waistcoat back
Cut 1 on fold
2cm (¾in)
9cm (3½in)
CB
To fold
55cm (21⅝in)
17cm (6⅝in)
18cm (7⅛in)
Woman's western-style waistcoat pocket
Cut 2

# Man's western-style waistcoat

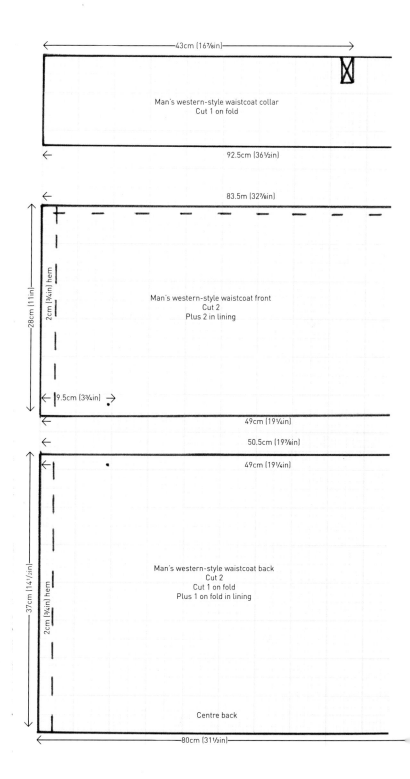

43cm (16⅞in)

Man's western-style waistcoat collar
Cut 1 on fold

92.5cm (36½in)

83.5m (32⅞in)

28cm (11in)

2cm (¾in) hem

Man's western-style waistcoat front
Cut 2
Plus 2 in lining

9.5cm (3¾in)

49cm (19¼in)

50.5cm (19⅞in)

49cm (19¼in)

37cm (14½in)

2cm (¾in) hem

Man's western-style waistcoat back
Cut 2
Cut 1 on fold
Plus 1 on fold in lining

Centre back

80cm (31½in)

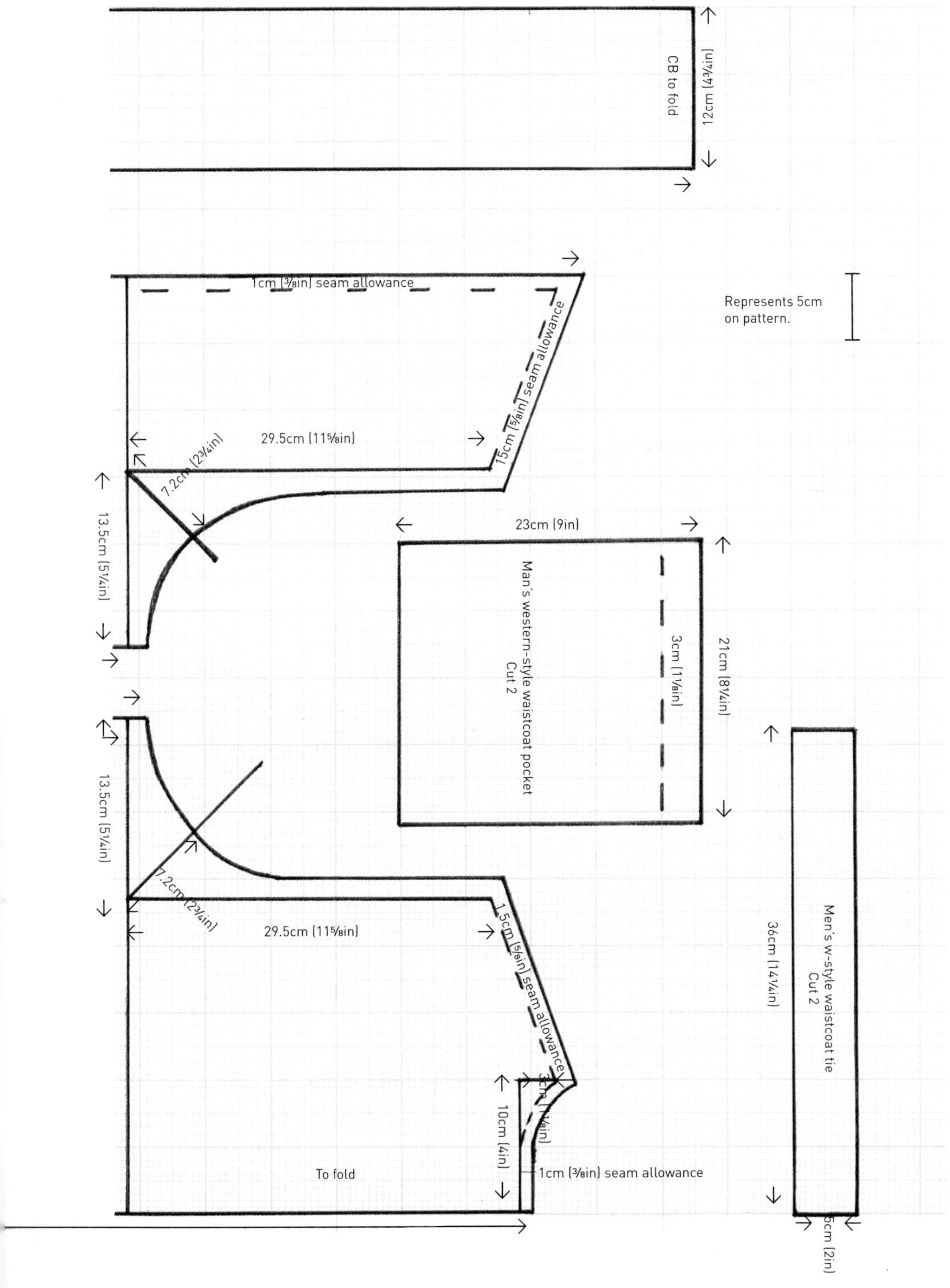

CB to fold
12cm (4¾in)
1cm (⅜in) seam allowance
Represents 5cm on pattern.
1.5cm (⅝in) seam allowance
29.5cm (11⅝in)
7.2cm (2¾in)
13.5cm (5¼in)
23cm (9in)
Man's western-style waistcoat pocket
Cut 2
3cm (1⅛in)
21cm (8¼in)
13.5cm (5¼in)
7.2cm (2¾in)
29.5cm (11⅝in)
1.5cm (⅝in) seam allowance
36cm (14¼in)
Men's w-style waistcoat tie
Cut 2
10cm (4in)
To fold
1cm (⅜in) seam allowance
5cm (2in)

# Hanten

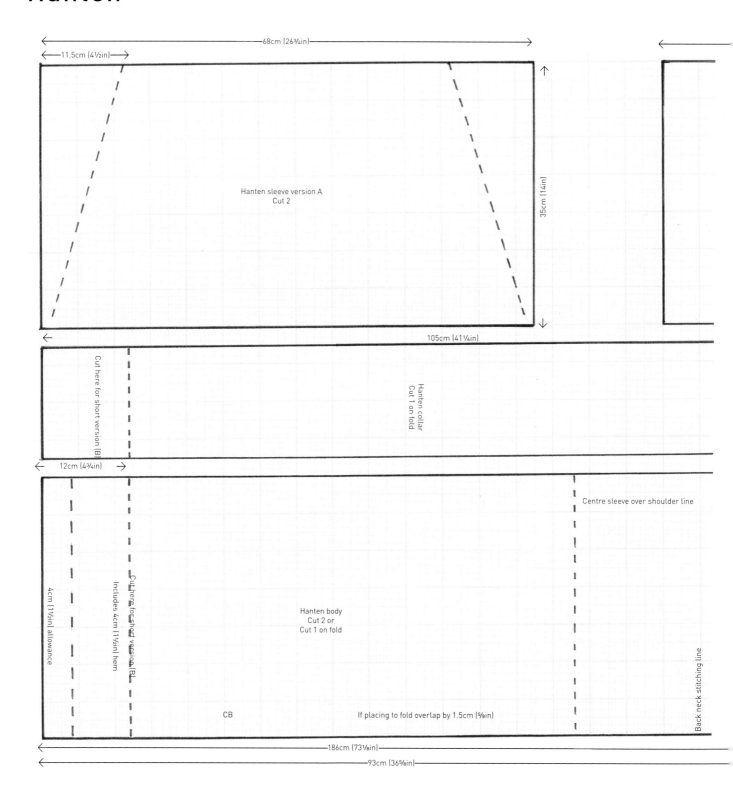

68cm (26¾in)

11.5cm (4½in)

Hanten sleeve version A
Cut 2

35cm (14in)

105cm (41¼in)

Cut here for short version (B)

Hanten collar
Cut 1 on fold

12cm (4¾in)

4cm (1½in) allowance

Includes 4cm (1½in) hem

Cut here for short version (B)

Centre sleeve over shoulder line

Hanten body
Cut 2 or
Cut 1 on fold

CB

If placing to fold overlap by 1.5cm (⅝in)

Back neck stitching line

186cm (73⅛in)

93cm (36⅝in)

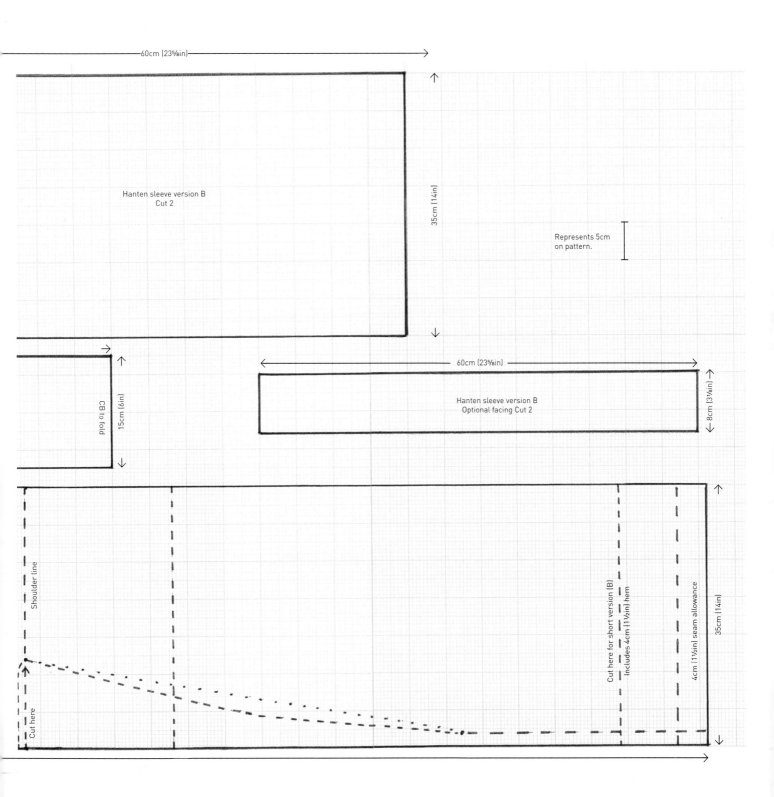

60cm (23⅝in)

Hanten sleeve version B
Cut 2

35cm (14in)

Represents 5cm
on pattern.

CB to fold

15cm (6in)

60cm (23⅝in)

Hanten sleeve version B
Optional facing Cut 2

8cm (3⅛in)

Shoulder line

Cut here

Cut here for short version (B)

Includes 4cm (1½in) hem

4cm (1½in) seam allowance

35cm (14in)

# Haori

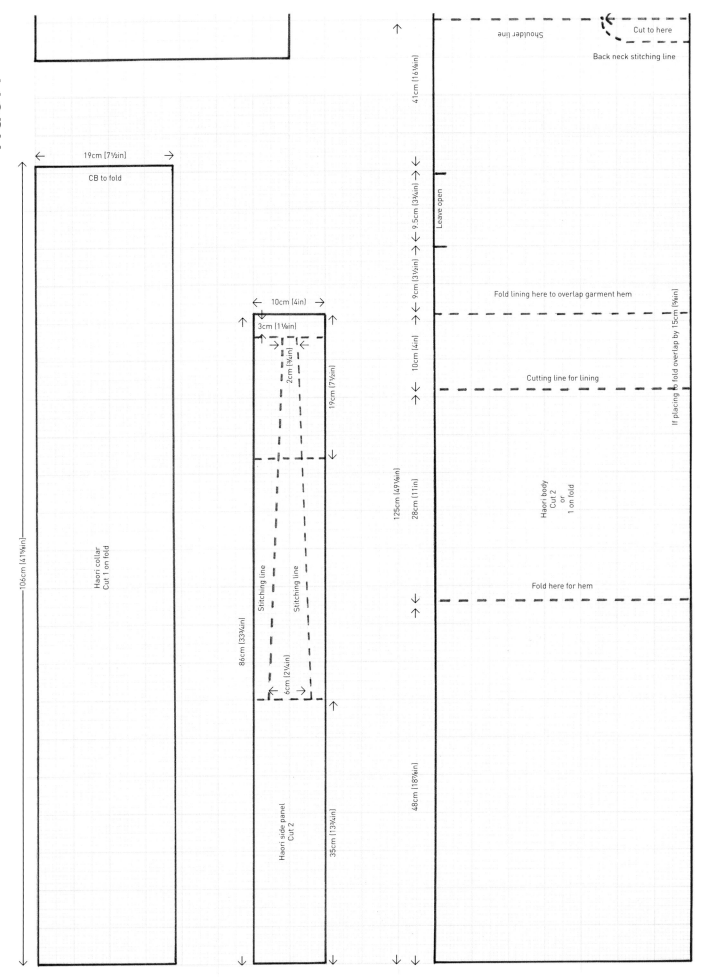

19cm [7½in]

CB to fold

Haori collar
Cut 1 on fold

106cm [41⅝in]

10cm [4in]

3cm [1⅛in]

2cm [¾in]

19cm [7½in]

Stitching line

Stitching line

86cm [33¾in]

6cm [2¼in]

Haori side panel
Cut 2

35cm [13¾in]

41cm [16⅛in]

9.5cm [3¾in]

Leave open

9cm [3½in]

10cm [4in]

125cm [49⅛in]

28cm [11in]

48cm [18⅞in]

Shoulder line

Cut to here

Back neck stitching line

Fold lining here to overlap garment hem

Cutting line for lining

If placing to fold overlap by 15cm [5⅞in]

Haori body
Cut 2
or
1 on fold

Fold here for hem

Shoulder line

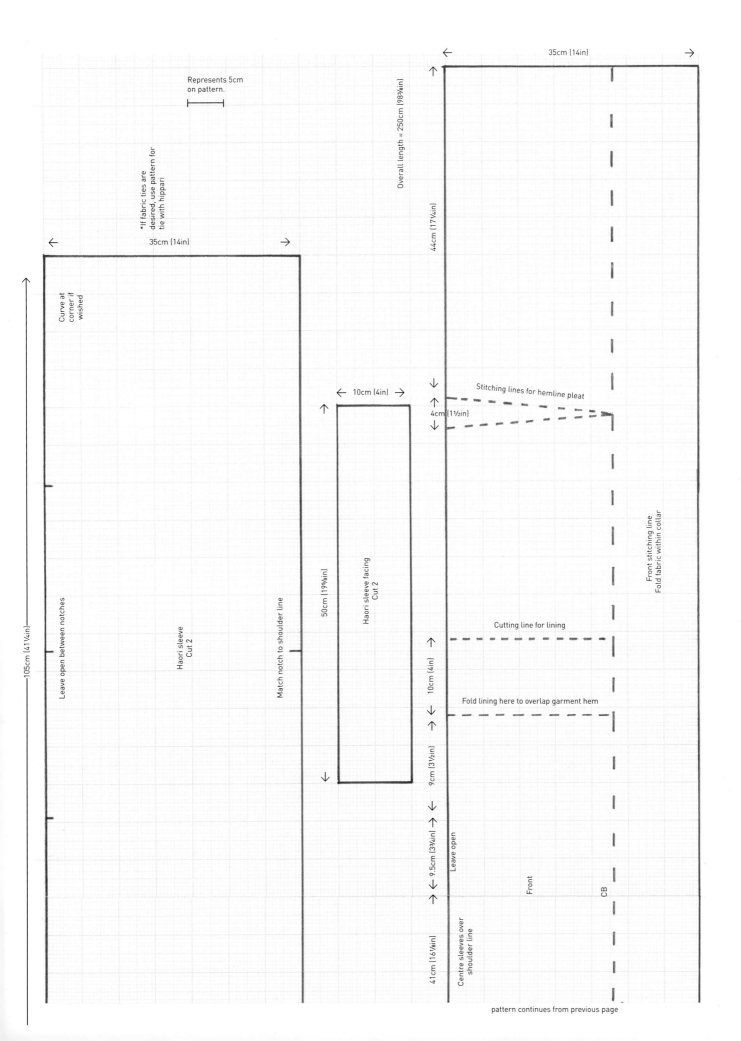

Represents 5cm on pattern.

*If fabric ties are desired, use pattern for tie with hippari

35cm (14in)

Curve at corner if wished

Leave open between notches

105cm (41¼in)

Haori sleeve
Cut 2

Match notch to shoulder line

Overall length = 250cm (98¾in)

35cm (14in)

44cm (17¼in)

Stitching lines for hemline pleat

10cm (4in)

4cm (1½in)

50cm (19⅝in)

Haori sleeve facing
Cut 2

Front stitching line
Fold fabric within collar

Cutting line for lining

10cm (4in)

Fold lining here to overlap garment hem

9cm (3½in)

9.5cm (3¾in)

Leave open

Front

CB

41cm (16⅛in)

Centre sleeves over shoulder line

pattern continues from previous page

# Mock Obi

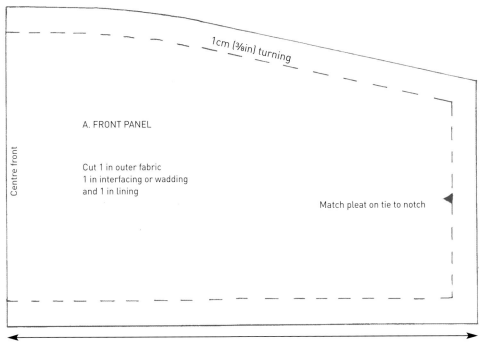

1cm (⅜in) turning

A. FRONT PANEL

Cut 1 in outer fabric
1 in interfacing or wadding
and 1 in lining

Centre front

Match pleat on tie to notch

Enlarge this line to measure 18cm (7in). Ensure both pattern pieces
are enlarged by the same amount.

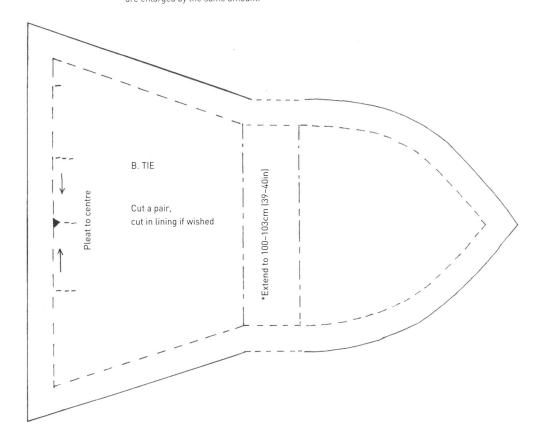

B. TIE

Cut a pair,
cut in lining if wished

Pleat to centre

*Extend to 100–103cm (39–40in)

# Japanese historical periods

| | | |
|---|---|---|
| JOMON | Prehistory–300BC | |
| YAYOI | 300 BC–AD 300 | |
| KOFUN | 300–552 | |
| ASUKA | 552–710 | time of Prince Shotoku, who named Japan |
| NARA | 710–794 | |
| HEIAN | 794–1185 | *The Tale of Genji* written during this time |
| KAMAKURA | 1185–1333 | |
| N & S COURTS | 1336–1392 | |
| MUROMACHI | 1392–1568 | 1549 arrival of Christianity |
| AZUCHI-MOMOYAMA | 1568–1600 | arrival of foreign traders |
| EDO | 1600–1867 | cultural isolation (late Tudor–mid-Victorian) |
| MEIJI | 1868–1912 | industrialization: the 'Meiji miracle' |
| TAISHO | 1912–1926 | |
| SHOWA | 1926–1989 | |
| HEISEI | 1989– | |

# Bibliography

Adachi, Fumi (translator). *Japanese Design Motifs.* Dover Pictorial Archive Series, New York, 1972

Chung, Young Y. *The Art of Oriental Embroidery: History, Aesthetics and Technique.* Bell and Hyman, London, 1980

Dalby, Liza. *Kimono: Fashioning Culture.* Vintage, a division of Random House, London, 2001

Dobson, Jenni. *Reader's Digest Patchwork, Quilting and Appliqué: The Complete Guide to All The Essential Techniques.* The Reader's Digest Association, 1998

Dower, John W. *The Elements of Japanese Design: A Handbook of Family Crests, Heraldry and Symbolism.* John Weatherill Inc, 1971

Liddell, Jill. *The Story of the Kimono.* E. P. Dutton, 1989

Liddell, Jill. *The Changing Seasons.* E. P. Dutton, 1992

Marshall, John. *Make Your Own Japanese Clothes: Patterns and Ideas for Modern Wear.* Kodansha International, Tokyo, New York, London, 1988

Nihon Vogue staff. *Sashiko: Traditional Japanese Quilt Designs.* Nihon Vogue, 1989.

Wada, Yoshiko, Mary Kellogg Rice, and Jane Barton. *Shibori: The Inventive Art of Japanese Shaped Resist Dyeing: Tradition, Techniques, Innovation.* Kodansha International Ltd, Tokyo, New York, London, 1983

Yang, Sunny, and Rochelle M. Narasin. *Textile Art of Japan.* Shufunotomo Co Ltd., Tokyo, 1989

# Picture credits

# Suppliers

For Japanese fabrics, embroidery threads etc:

**Euro-Japan Links Ltd**
32 Nant Road
Child's Hill
London NW2 2AT
Tel: + 44 (0)20 8201 9324
E-mail: eurojpn@aol.com

For silk:

**The Silk Route**
Cross Cottage
Cross Lane
Frimley Green
Surrey GU16 6LN
Tel: + 44 (0)1252 835781
Website: www.thesilkroute.co.uk
E-mail: hilary@thesilkroute.co.uk

For a wide range of silks for dyeing/printing & other supplies, free catalogue:

**Whaley's (Bradford) Ltd**
Hams Court
Great Horton
Bradford
West Yorkshire BD7 4EQ
Tel: + 44 (0)1274 576718
Fax: + 44 (0)1274 521309
Website: www.whaleys-bradford.ltd.uk
E-mail:whaleys@btinternet.com

# Index

# making
# kimono
# & japanese clothes

Jenni Dobson

Batsford

**Dedication**

This book is dedicated to the memory of my mother, Pat Allen. Some of her fabrics and threads, together with her Bernina, helped to make this book possible, even though she did not live to see it. Thank you, Mum!

**Author's acknowledgements**

Influences on a book such as this obviously come from many directions, some unrecognized because they are so subtle. My longstanding friend and mentor, Jill Liddell, author of *The Story of the Kimono*, has been the source of much of my background knowledge about Japan over the years – and a fountain of encouragement.

I also wish to acknowledge the comprehensive work by John Marshall, *Make Your Own Japanese Clothes* (Kodansha, 1988), which I purchased in the early 1990s. My book does not presume to copy this work, but rather to offer a simpler level of making and to emphasize the decorative possibilities of Japanese garment forms.

In this aim I was much encouraged and supported by Mary and Shiro Tamakoshi of Euro-Japan Links, London, England, who loaned most of the source garments from which my patterns were derived and who gave generous permission for photography. The lovely light blue haori, source garment in Chapter 8, is a treasured gift from my Japanese friend Atsuko Ohta of Patchwork Quilt Tsushin, Tokyo. I am indebted to friends Sue Barry and Minou Button-de Groote for their garments and Sue in particular for her advice on silk painting. Thanks also to Dianne Huck of the British *Patchwork and Quilting* magazine for permission to rework an article on shibori, first printed in the magazine, for the benefit of this book.

I must mention Pat Allen, my mother, and Mary Dale, maternal grandmother, for without their skills and knowledge in my childhood days, I would not be the needlewoman that I am. Finally, a big thank you to my husband and family for their support and tolerance of my stitching career!

First published 2004
Reprinted 2004, 2005

Copyright © Jenni Dobson 2004

Volume © B T Batsford 2004

The right of Jenni Dobson to be identified as Author of this work has been asserted by her in accordance with the Copyright, Designs and Patents Act 1988.

0 7134 8903 0

A CIP record for this book is available from the British Library.

Design by Lee-May Lim

Printed in Malaysia
for the publishers

B T Batsford
The Chrysalis Building
Bramley Road
London W10 6SP
www.chrysalisbooks.co.uk

An imprint of **Chrysalis** Books Group plc

Distributed in the United States and Canada by Sterling Publishing Co.,
387 Park Avenue South, New York, NY 10016, USA